CHUCK

PALAHNIUK

STRANGER

THAN

FICTION

{True Stories}

DOUBLEDAY NEW YORK LONDON TORONTO SYDNEY AUCKLAND

PUBLISHED BY DOUBLEDAY
a division of Random House, Inc.

DOUBLEDAY and the portrayal of an anchor with a dolphin are
registered trademarks of Random House, Inc.

Book design by Dana Leigh Treglia

Library of Congress Cataloging-in-Publication Data

Palahniuk, Chuck.
Stranger than fiction : true stories / Chuck Palahniuk.—1st ed.
p.   cm.
I. Title.

PS3566.A4554S77 2004
813'.54—dc22

ISBN 0-385-50448-9

Some of the stories in this book have appeared, in slightly different form, in the
following publications: "Escort" in *Bikini Review*; "My Life as a Dog," "Frontiers,"
"In Her Own Words," and "The Lip Enhancer" in *Black Book*; "Why Isn't He
Budging?" in *Boswell*; "Testy Festy," "Where Meat Comes From," "Monkey
Think, Monkey Do," and "Reading Yourself" in *Gear*; "The Lady" in *The
Independent*; "Not Chasing Amy" in *L.A. Weekly*; "Consolation Prizes" in the
Los Angeles Times; "The People Can" in *NEST*; "Demolition" in *Playboy*;
"Brinksmanship" in *Speakeasy*; and "Almost California" in *The Stranger.*

PRINTED IN THE UNITED STATES OF AMERICA

June 2004
First Edition

1   3   5   7   9   10   8   6   4   2

CONTENTS

For Mick and Chick
and Chimp

{Fact and Fiction: An Introduction}

If you haven't already noticed, all my books are about a lonely person looking for some way to connect with other people.

In a way, that is the opposite of the American Dream: to get so rich you can rise above the rabble, all those people on the freeway or, worse, *the bus*. No, the dream is a big house, off alone somewhere. A penthouse, like Howard Hughes. Or a mountaintop castle, like William Randolph Hearst. Some lovely isolated nest where you can invite only the rabble you like. An environment you can control, free from conflict and pain. Where you rule.

Whether it's a ranch in Montana or basement apartment with ten thousand DVDs and high-speed Internet access, it never fails. We get there, and we're alone. And we're lonely.

After we're miserable enough—like the narrator in his *Fight Club* condo, or the narrator isolated by her own beautiful face in *Invisible Monsters*—we destroy our lovely nest and force ourselves back into the larger world. In so many ways, that's also how you write a novel. You plan and research. You spend time alone, building this lovely world where you control, control, control everything. You let the telephone ring. The emails pile up. You stay in your story world until you destroy it. Then you come back to be with other people.

If your story world sells well enough, you get to go on book tour. Do interviews. *Really* be with people. A lot of people. People, until you're sick of people. Until you crave the idea of escaping, getting away to a . . .

To another lovely story world.

And so it goes. Alone. Together. Alone. Together.

Chances are, if you're reading this, you know this cycle. Reading a book is not a group activity. Not like going to a movie or a concert. This is the lonely end of the spectrum.

Every story in this book is about being with other people. Me being with people. Or people being together.

For the castle builders, it's about flying a stone flag so grand it attracts people with the same dream.

For the combine-demolition folks, it's about finding a way to get together, a social structure with rules and goals and roles for people to fill while they rebuild their community by crashing farm equipment.

For Marilyn Manson, it's about a kid from the Midwest who can't swim, suddenly moved to Florida, where social life is lived in the ocean. Here, that kid is still trying to connect with people.

These are all nonfiction stories and essays I wrote between novels. In my own cycle, it goes: Fact. Fiction. Fact. Fiction.

The one drawback to writing is the being alone. The writing part. The lonely-garret part. In people's imagination, that's the difference between a writer and a journalist. The journalist, the newspaper reporter, is always rushing, hunting, meeting people, digging up facts. Cooking a story. The journalist writes surrounded by people, and always on deadline. Crowded and hurried. Exciting and fun.

The journalist writes to connect you to the larger world. A conduit.

But a *writer* writer is different. Anybody who writes fiction is—people imagine—alone. Maybe because fiction seems to connect you to only the voice of one other person. Maybe because reading is something we do *alone*. It's a pastime that seems to split us away from others.

The journalist researches a story. The novelist imagines it.

What's funny is, you'd be amazed at the amount of time a novelist has to spend with people in order to create this single lonely voice. This seemingly isolated world.

It's hard to call any of my novels "fiction."

Most of the reason I write is because once a week it brought me together with other people. This was in a workshop taught by a published writer—Tom Spanbauer—around his kitchen table on Thursday nights. At the time, most of my friendships were based on proximity: neighbors or coworkers. Those people you know only because, well, you're stuck sitting next to them every day.

The funniest person I know, Ina Gebert, calls coworkers your "air family."

The problem with proximity friends is, they move away. They quit or get fired.

It wasn't until a writing workshop that I discovered the idea of friendships based on a shared passion. Writing. Or theater.

Or music. Some shared vision. A mutual quest that would keep you together with other people who valued this vague, intangible skill you valued. These are friendships that outlast jobs and evictions. This steady, regular Thursday-night gabfest was the only incentive to keep me writing during the years when writing didn't pay a dime. Tom and Suzy and Monica and Steven and Bill and Cory and Rick. We fought and praised each other. And it was enough.

My pet theory about *Fight Club*'s success is that the story presented a structure for people to be together. People want to see new ways for connecting. Look at books like *How to Make an American Quilt* and *The Divine Secrets of the Ya-Ya Sisterhood* and *The Joy Luck Club*. These are all books that present a structure—making a quilt or playing mah-jongg—that allows people to be together and share their stories. All these books are short stories bound together by a shared activity. Of course, they're all women's stories. We don't see a lot of new models for male social interaction. There's sports. Barn raisings. That's about it.

And now there's fight clubs. For better or worse.

Before I started writing *Fight Club*, I worked as a volunteer at a charity hospice. My job was to drive people to appointments and support-group meetings. There, they'd sit around with other people in a church basement, comparing symptoms and doing New Age exercises. Those meetings were uncomfortable because no matter how I tried to hide, people always assumed I had the disease they had. There was no discreet way to say I was just observing, a tourist waiting to take my charge back to the hospice. So I started telling myself a story about a guy who haunted terminal illness support groups to feel better about his own pointless life.

In so many ways, these places—support groups, twelve-step

recovery groups, demolition derbies—they've come to serve the role that organized religion used to. We used to go to church to reveal the worst aspects of ourselves, our sins. To tell our stories. To be recognized. To be forgiven. And to be redeemed, accepted back into our community. This ritual was our way to stay connected to people, and to resolve our anxiety before it could take us so far from humanity that we would be lost.

In these places I found the truest stories. In support groups. In hospitals. Anywhere people had nothing left to lose, that's where they told the most truth.

While writing *Invisible Monsters*, I'd call telephone sex numbers and ask people to tell me their dirtiest stories. You can just call and say: "Hey, everybody, I'm looking for *hot* brother-sister incest stories, let's hear yours!" or "Tell me about your dirtiest, filthiest cross-dressing fantasy!" and you'll be taking notes for hours. Because it's only sound, it's like an obscene radio show. Some people are terrible actors, but some will break your heart.

On one call, a kid talked about being blackmailed into having sex with a policeman who threatened to have his parents charged with abuse and neglect. The policeman gave the kid gonorrhea, and the parents he was trying to save . . . they threw him out to live on the street. Telling his story, near the end the kid started to cry. If he was lying, it was a magnificent performance. A tiny one-on-one piece of theater. If it was a story, it was still a *great* story.

So of course I used it in the book.

The world is made of people telling stories. Look at the stock market. Look at fashion. And any long story, any novel, is just a combination of short stories.

While researching my fourth book, *Choke*, I sat in on sex-addict talk therapy sessions, twice each week for six months. Wednesday and Friday nights.

In so many ways, these rap sessions weren't much different than the Thursday-night writers' workshop I attended. Both groups were just people telling their stories. The sexaholics might've been a little less concerned about "craft," but they still told their stories of anonymous bathroom sex and prostitutes with enough skill to get a good reaction from their audience. Many of these people had talked in meetings for so many years that hearing them, you heard a great soliloquy. A brilliant actor playing him- or herself. A one-person monologue that showed an instinct for slowly revealing key information, creating dramatic tension, setting up payoffs and completely enrolling the listener.

For *Choke*, I also sat with Alzheimer's patients as a volunteer. My role was just to ask them about the old photographs each patient kept in a box in their closet, to try and spur their memory. It was a job the nursing staff didn't have time to do. And, again, it was about telling stories. One subplot of *Choke* came together as, day by day, each patient would look at the same photo, but tell a different story about it. One day, the beautiful bare-breasted woman would be their wife. The next day, she was some woman they met in Mexico while serving in the navy. The next day, the woman was an old friend from work. What struck me is . . . they *had to* create a story to explain who she was. Even if they'd forgotten, they'd never admit it. A faulty well-told story was always better than admitting they didn't recognize this woman.

Telephone sex lines, illness support groups, twelve-step groups, all these places are schools for learning how to *tell* a story effectively. Out loud. To people. Not just to look for ideas, but how to *perform*.

We live our lives according to stories. About being Irish or being black. About working hard or shooting heroin. Being male or female. And we spend our lives looking for evidence—facts and proof—that support our story. As a writer, you just recognize that part of human nature. Each time you create a character, you look at the world as that character, looking for the details that make that reality the one true reality.

Like a lawyer arguing a case in a courtroom, you become an advocate who wants the reader to accept the truth of your character's worldview. You want to give the reader a break from their own life. From their own life story.

This is how I create a character. I tend to give each character an education and a skill set that limits how they see the world. A house cleaner sees the world as an endless series of stains to remove. A fashion model sees the world as a series of rivals for public attention. A failed medical student sees nothing but the moles and twitches that might be the early signs of a terminal illness.

During this same period when I started writing, friends and I started a weekly tradition we called "Game Night." Every Sunday evening we'd meet to play party games, like charades. Some nights we'd never start the game. All we needed was the excuse, and sometimes a structure, to be together. If I was stuck in my writing, looking for a new way to develop a theme, I'd do what I'd later call "crowd seeding." I'd throw out a topic of conversation, maybe tell a quick funny story and prompt people to tell their own versions.

Writing *Survivor*, I'd bring up the topic of cleaning hints, and people would provide them for hours. For *Choke*, it was coded security announcements. For *Diary*, I told stories about what I'd found, or left, sealed inside the walls of houses I'd worked on. Hearing my handful of stories, my friends told theirs. And their guests told their stories. And within one evening, I had enough for a book.

In this way, even the lonely act of writing becomes an excuse to be around people. In turn, the people fuel the storytelling.

Alone. Together. Fact. Fiction. It's a cycle.

Comedy. Tragedy. Light. Dark. They define each other.

It works, but only if you don't get stuck too long in any one place.

PEOPLE TOGETHER

{Testy Festy}

A pretty blonde tilts her cowboy hat farther back on her head. This is so she can deep-throat a cowboy without her hat brim hitting him in the gut. This is on a stage, in a crowded bar. Both of them are naked and smeared with chocolate pudding and whipped cream. This they call the "Co-Ed Body Painting Contest." The stage is red carpet. The lights, fluorescent. The crowd chants, "We want head! We want head!"

The cowboy sprays whipped cream in the crack of the blonde's ass and eats it out. The blonde masturbates him with a handful of chocolate pudding. Another couple take the stage and the man licks pudding out of the woman's shaved pussy. A girl with a brown ponytail in a halter top sucks off a kid with an uncut dick.

This is while the crowd sings "You've Lost That Loving Feeling."

As the girl leaves the stage, one of her girlfriends shouts, "You *sucked* him, you little bitch!"

The crowd is packed in, smoking cigars, drinking Rainier Beer, drinking Schmidt's and Miller, eating deep-fried bull gonads dipped in ranch dressing. You smell sweat, and when somebody farts, the chocolate pudding doesn't look like pudding anymore.

This is the Rock Creek Lodge Testicle Festival just getting started.

This is some fifteen miles south of Missoula, Montana, where this same weekend drag queens from a dozen states meet to crown their Empress. This is why hundreds of Christians have come into town, to sit on street corners in lawn chairs and point at the drag queens strutting in miniskirts, and at the fifteen thousand leather bikers roaring through town on choppers. The Christians point and shout, "Demon! I can see you, demon! You are not hiding!"

For just this one weekend, the first weekend in September, Missoula is the center of the frigging universe.

At the Rock Creek Lodge, people climb the "Stairway to Heaven," the outdoor stage, all weekend to do, well . . . you name it.

A stone's throw to the east, trucks go by on Interstate 90, blowing their air horns as the girls onstage hook their legs over the railings and pump their shaved pussies in the air. Half a stone's throw to the west, the Burlington Northern freight trains slow to get a better look and blow their sirens.

"I built the stage with thirteen steps," says festival founder Rod Jackson. "It could always be a gallows."

Except that it's painted red, the stage *looks* like a gallows.

During the women's wet T-shirt contest, the stage surrounded by bikers and college kids and yuppies and truckers, skinny cowboys and rednecks, a blonde in clunky high heels hooks one leg over the stage railing and squats low on her other leg so the crowd can reach up and finger her.

The crowd chants, "Beaver! Beaver! Beaver!"

A blonde with short hair and a ring through her labia grabs the garden hose from the wet T-shirt organizer. She douches with the hose and squats at the edge of the stage, spraying the crowd.

Two brunettes suck each other's wet breasts and French kiss. Another woman leads a German shepherd up on stage. She leans back, pumping her hips as she holds the dog's mouth between her legs.

A couple in buckskin costumes climb the stage and strip. They copulate in a lot of different positions while the crowd chants, "Fuck her! Fuck her! Fuck her!"

A blond college girl balances with both feet up on the stage railing and slowly lowers her shaved pussy onto the smiling face of the contest organizer, Gary "the Hoser," while the crowd sings "London Bridge Is Falling Down."

In the souvenir shop, naked sunburned people stand in line to buy souvenir T-shirts ($11.95). Men in black Testicle Festival thongs ($5.95) buy hand-carved dildos called "Montana Wood Peckers" ($15.00). On the outdoor stage, under the big Montana sun, with the traffic and trains honking, a wood pecker disappears into a nude woman.

The line of souvenir shoppers edges past a barrel full of walking sticks, each stick a yard long, leathery brown, and sticky to the touch. A good-sized woman waiting to buy a T-shirt says, "Those are dried bull dicks." She says how you can get the penises from butcher shops or slaughterhouses, then stretch and dry them. You finish them like furniture, with a light sanding and many coats of varnish.

A naked man standing behind her in line, his whole body just as brown and leathery as the walking sticks, he asks if the woman has ever actually made one of the sticks.

The good-sized woman blushes and says, "Hell no. I'm too embarrassed to ask the butcher for a bull dick . . ."

And the leathery man says, "A butcher'd probably think you'd use it on yourself."

And everyone standing in line—the woman included—laughs and laughs.

Every time a woman squats on stage, a forest of arms comes up, each hand holding an orange disposable camera, and the click of shutters is thick as crickets.

A disposable camera costs $15.99 here.

During the "Men's Bare Chest Contest" the crowd chants "Dick and balls! Dick and balls!" as the drunk bikers and cowboys and college kids from Montana State stand in line to strip on stage and swing their parts over the crowd. A Brad Pitt look-alike pumps his erection in the air. A woman reaches between his legs from behind and masturbates him until he turns suddenly, slapping her in the face with his hard-on.

The woman grabs hold and drags him off the stage.

The old men sit on logs, drinking beer and throwing rocks at the fiberglass porta-potties where the women pee. The men pee anywhere.

By now the parking lot is paved with crushed beer cans.

Inside the Rock Creek Lodge, women crawl under a life-sized statue of a bull, to kiss its scrotum for good luck.

On a dirt track running down one edge of the property, motorcycles race in a "Ball Biting" contest. Sitting on the back of each bike, a woman must snap her teeth on a hanging bull testicle and tear off a mouthful as her male driver races over the course.

Away from the main crowd, a trail of men leads back into the field of camp trailers and tents, where two women are getting dressed. The two describe themselves as "just a couple regular girls from White Fish, with regular jobs and everything."

One says, "Did you hear that applause? We won. We definitely won."

A drunk young guy says, "So what do you win?"

And the girl says, "There's no prize or anything, but we're the definite winners."

{Where Meat Comes From}

It takes a couple hours before you notice what's wrong with everyone.

It's their ears. It's as if you've landed on some planet where almost everybody's ears are mangled and crushed, melted and shrunken. It's not the first thing you notice about people, but after you notice it, it's the only thing you see.

"To most wrestlers, cauliflower ear is like a tattoo," says Justin Petersen. "It's like a status symbol. It's kind of looked on with pride in the community. It means you've put in the time."

"That's just from getting in there and brawling, getting in there and getting your ears rubbed a lot," says William R. Groves. "What happens is, as you rub and rub and rub, the abrasion, the cartilage separates from the skin, and in that separation, blood and fluid fills it up. After a while, it drains out, but the calcium will solidify on the cartilage. A lot of wrestlers see it as a kind of badge of wrestling, a necessary badge of wrestling."

Sean Harrington says, "It's like a stalactite or something. Slowly blood trickles in there and hardens. It gets injured again, and a little more blood trickles in and hardens, and slowly it's unrecognizable anymore. Some guys definitely feel that way, that it's a badge of courage, a badge of honor."

"I think it's very much a badge of honor," says Sara Levin. "You know somebody's a wrestler. It's another one of those things that makes someone else an equal to you. And a bond. Part of the grind. The ears. It's just part of the game. It's the nature of the sport, like scars, battle wounds."

Petersen says, "I had one teammate who, before he'd go to bed, he'd sit there and punch his ear for ten minutes. He wanted cauliflower ear so bad."

"I've drained mine a lot," says Joe Calavitta. "I got syringes, and when they blew up, I kept draining them. They fill up. They fill up with blood. As long as you keep draining them before the blood hardens, you can keep it down, pretty much. You can get it done by a doctor, but you'd have to go in all the time, so you just get your own syringes and do it."

Petersen, Groves, Harrington, and Calavitta, they're amateur wrestlers.

Levin is the Men's Event Coordinator for USA Wrestling, the national governing body for amateur wrestling.

What happens on this page isn't wrestling, it's writing. At best, this is a postcard from a hot, dry weekend in Waterloo,

Iowa. Where meat comes from. From the North Regional Olympic Trials, the first step, where for twenty dollars any man can compete for a chance on the U.S. Olympic Wrestling Team.

The Nationals are over, so are the other regionals. This is the last chance to qualify for the finals.

These men, some are here to wrestle other high school "Junior" level wrestlers now that the regular season is over.

For some of these men, who range in age from seventeen to forty-one, this will be their last shot at the Olympics. As Levin says, "You're going to see the end of a lot of careers here."

Everybody here will tell you about amateur wrestling.

It's the ultimate sport, they'll tell you. It's the oldest sport. It's the purest sport. The toughest sport.

It's a sport under attack from men and women alike.

It's a dying sport.

It's a cult. It's a club. It's a drug. It's a fraternity. It's a family.

For all of these people, amateur wrestling is a misunderstood sport.

"Track and field, you run from here to there. Basketball, you put the ball in the hoop," says three-time world champion Kevin Jackson. "Wrestling has two different styles, as well as folkstyle and collegiate styles of wrestling, which gives you so many rules that the general public cannot follow it."

"You don't have the cheerleaders running around, confetti falling from the ceiling, and Jack Nicholson in the bleachers," says former college and army team wrestler Butch Wingett. "You might have a bunch of grizzled old guys who might be farmers or were maybe laid off from the John Deere plant."

"I think that wrestlers are misjudged a lot," says Lee Pritts, who wrestles freestyle at 54 kilograms. "It's actually a classy sport.

And a lot of times it's kinda considered barbaric. Wrestling gets a lot of bad publicity."

"Right now, people just don't understand the sport," says Jackson, "and if you don't understand something or know who might compete in it, you won't watch."

"People don't give the sport its respect because they're, like, 'Oh, it's just two guys rolling around,' and I think that's wrong," says three-time NCAA wrestler Tyrone Davis, who wrestles Greco-Roman at 130 kilograms. "It's more than just two guys rolling around. Basically, wrestling's like life. You got a lot of decisions out there. *The mat* is your life."

When you fly into Waterloo, Iowa, the city looks exactly like the map on its website, flat and cut with freeways. At the Young Arena, near the dry, empty downtown, all day before weigh-ins, wrestlers stop in to ask if there's a sauna in town. Where's the scale? The Young Arena is where elderly people go on weekdays to walk around and around the air-conditioned indoor track.

Wrestlers will lose up to a pound a minute during a seven-minute match. The training stories they tell include running in-flight "laps," back and forth in jetliners, despite the crew's protests. Then doing chin-ups in the jetliner's galley area. An old trick for high school wrestlers is to ask to go to the bathroom during every class, and then doing chin-ups on the toilet stall walls, letting the sharp edge along the top cut calluses into their hands. They talk about running up and down the bleachers, past angry fans during basketball games, in order to make their competitive weight the next day.

In 1998, Wingett says, three college wrestlers died of dehydration trying to cut weight while taking the supplement Creatine.

"I don't think there's any more grueling or tougher sport to train in," says Kevin Jackson. "By going through that, it's a humbling experience. You do get beat in the practice room. You do get fatigued running the track or running the stadium stairs."

Wingett talks about long runs in the middle of summer where three wrestlers take turns, two chasing a pickup truck that the third drives with the windows rolled up and the heater cranked.

"You get it down to a system," says Justin Petersen, who at seventeen years old has had his nose broken more than fifteen times. "You think: 'I can have *this* carton of milk, I can have *this* bagel, and I will have sweated it off by *this* time of the day, at which time I can have *this* sip of water and still make weight.' You have it down exact."

Lee Pritts and Mark Strickland, a 76-kilogram freestyle wrestler with "Strick" tattooed on his arm, have brought their own stationary bikes into town and are sweating off the weight in room 232 of the Hartland Inn. A third friend, Nick Feldman, is here for moral support and to massage them when their bodies get so dehydrated that their muscles cramp.

Feldman, a former college wrestler who drove down from Mitchell, South Dakota, says, "Wrestling's like a club where once you get in, you can't get out."

"You see the other athletes in the schools, the basketball players and the football players, they'll talk about how 'wrestling's not *that* tough,' but then they join the team, and they quit within the week," says Sean Harrington, who's been training at Colorado Springs for the past six months in order to compete in freestyle at 76 kilograms.

He says, "We always have such pride in the fact that we

work harder than everybody else, and we get no recognition to speak of. I mean, there's no fans here. Most of them are parents. It's not a popular sport."

"When I was in college I cried a lot just because it was so hard, and I was never very good," says Ken Bigley, twenty-four, who started wrestling in first grade and now coaches at Ohio State University. "I asked myself a lot of times why I did it. One analogy I like to use is it's like a drug. You get addicted to it. Sometimes you know—you know it's not good for you, especially emotionally, some of those tough practices or bad competitions, but you just keep coming back for it. If I didn't need it, I wouldn't be here. You don't make money off it. You don't get any glory off it. It's just searching for the high, I guess."

Sean Harrington says, "I've been wrestling so long that I don't remember what pain was like before wrestling."

Says Lee Pritts, twenty-six, a coach at the University of Missouri, "It's kind of weird. You get in the shower after a tournament and your face is usually banged up from wrestling all day, and the water running over it gives you a little burn, but if you take a week off you miss it. You miss the pain. After a week off, you're ready to go back because you miss the pain."

The pain is maybe one reason why the stands are almost empty.

Amateur wrestling isn't easy to watch. It can be a flesh-and-blood demolition derby.

During the first minute of his first match last Christmas, Sean Harrington broke his wrist.

Keith Wilson's injuries include his shoulder, elbow, knee, his right ankle, and a herniated disk between C5 and C6 of his spine. Seven surgeries, total.

At home in a jar full of alcohol, junior-level wrestler Mike

Engelmann from Spencer, Iowa, keeps a translucent sliver of cartilage that surgeons removed from the meniscus of his knee. It's his good-luck charm. He's been stitched up nine times.

About his nose, Ken Bigley says, "Sometimes it's pointing left. Sometimes it's pointing right."

A medic in an orange "Sports Injury Center" T-shirt says, "Ringworm is unbelievably common among these guys."

One of the oldest rules, he says, is that wrestlers have to get down and wipe up their own blood with a spray bottle of bleach.

"His grandparents will say all the time, 'This is nuts,'" says software engineer David Rodrigues, here with his seventeen-year-old son, Chris, a four-time Georgia State champion who placed fifth in the world in the Youth Games in Moscow last year.

"There's been the injuries," he says, listing them off. "Hyperextended knee, hyperextended elbow, he had a slight tear in a back muscle, a broken hand, broken finger, broken toe, sprained knee, but we've seen worse. We've seen kids carried out on stretchers. Broken collarbones, broken arm, broken leg, broken neck. God forbid, we had a kid in Georgia whose neck was broken. Those are the kind of injuries you pray that never happen, but at the same token we all understand that's the nature of the sport."

"And my broken tooth," his son, Chris, says.

And David Rodrigues says, "His tooth broke off and it was in the kid's head, sticking out of the kid's head."

About Chris's mother, David Rodrigues says, "My wife will only go to a couple tournaments a year. She'll go to State and she'll go to Nationals, but she won't go to a lot because she's afraid of injuries. She doesn't want to be there when one happens."

Chris's front teeth are bonded now.

In a few more days, Chris Rodrigues will break his jaw in the Junior World Team Trials.

Justin Petersen says, "There's a picture of me after the state tournament my sophomore year. I had hit someone's knee with my face so one side of my face was all swollen, and the other side of my face I had mat burn. It's nasty. It seeps and scabs and the scabs keep breaking every time you move your facial muscles. And my nose, I'd broken *that* again, so I had a cotton ball up my nose. And I'd sprained my shoulder again, so I had a big ice pack up to my shoulder. I'd just finished wrestling my last match and someone took a picture of me."

Timothy O'Rourke, who's wrestling today for the first time in nineteen years, is here without his wife. "She doesn't want to see me get hurt," he says. "Rolling around with the big boys . . . She's afraid she's going to see me get hurt, so she stayed at the hotel."

For Greco-Roman wrestler Phil Lanzatella, it was his wife who first noticed his injury and saved his life.

"I was going to Sweden/Norway, and my wife was putting her head to my chest, hugging me," he says. "I'd just gotten back from the Olympic Training Center. And she's about five-three, and she said, 'Your heart sounds like it's making a funny sound.' She said, 'You'd better get checked out.' So I went to the emergency room."

It was a torn heart valve.

Lanzatella says, "To make a long story short, I went in on Sunday night and they told me on Tuesday of that next week that I'd need immediate open-heart surgery. The only thing they could surmise is that it was from wrestling. One of the top surgeons in the world, the one who did my surgery, said he'd never seen an injury like it in his career. If you tear a valve like that, the analogy is hitting the steering wheel of a car, head-on, at sixty miles an hour."

The heart valve was torn in three places—in a V shape, with another tear horizontally across the midpoint of the V—forcing Lanzatella's heart to pump five times faster than normal to keep up.

This was in February of 1997. Phil Lanzatella had qualified for the Olympic trials every year since 1980, when he was on top, still a teenager, but already a world-class wrestler, dating Water Mondale's daughter and headed for the Olympics in Moscow. The Olympics we boycotted that year. Now, for Phil the options were a mechanical valve, a pig heart valve, or a re-covered human valve. The recovered valve was the choice that would let him still compete.

After that, he started helping coach at local colleges and high schools. He started feeling good, getting a little more active.

"I didn't tell my wife. I came home one day and said, 'Hey, Mel, what do you think about me wrestling?' and she said, 'Yeah, okay, if you want to be single. I'm not going through *that* again.' But she got used to the idea."

They've been married fifteen years.

Finally, Melody Lanzatella said, "If you're going to do this, then you're going to win."

So far, Phil hasn't. He didn't make it in the South Regionals.

"I took tenth in the Nationals, top eight qualifying, in Las Vegas. In Tulsa," he says, "my hotel van broke down, and I missed weigh-ins. I got stuck on the highway. So this is really it. This is it, literally."

So for Phil Lanzatella, thirty-seven, this is his last shot at the Olympics after decades of training and competition.

It's the last shot for Sheldon Kim, twenty-nine, from Orange

County, California, who works full-time as an inventory analyst and is here with his wife, Sasha, and their three-year-old, Michaela, and who is busy right now trying to drop two extra pounds in the last half-hour before weigh-ins are over.

It's the last shot for Trevor Lewis, thirty-three, the comptroller at Penn State with a master's degree in engineering and architecture, who's here with his father.

It's the last shot for Keith Wilson, thirty-three, who has a baby boy due in two weeks and practices two or three times every day as part of the army's World Class Athlete program.

It's the last shot for Michael Jones, thirty-eight, of Southfield, Michigan, whose first film project, *Revelations: The Movie*, is about to begin production.

Jones says, "My body just can't go through another four years of wrestling guys like this. Like I say, my knees are starting to buckle. My back is starting to really get to me now. I don't want to get to around fifty years old and be bent over with a cane. This will definitely be my last Olympics."

It's the last shot for former college wrestler Timothy O'Rourke, forty-one, who last wrestled in 1980 and says, "I saw something on the Internet and thought, 'What the hell, I'll give it a shot.' "

Despite everything at stake, the mood is less like a fighting tournament than a family reunion.

Keith Wilson is here from the Olympic Training Center in Colorado Springs to compete as a 76-kilogram Greco-Roman wrestler.

"I don't hold anything in," he says. "I'm happy all the time. And if I get stressed, I have an okay outlet. I can just come here and beat the shit out of someone and I won't get in trouble for it. When you wrestle, it's for blood, but when you walk off the mat, you're friends again."

"It's almost like a family," says Chris Rodrigues. "You know everyone. I know everyone. You meet people you know, and everyone gets to know each other, hanging out at the big national tournaments. The Junior Nationals and the Nationals, every year. It's like a big connection to everyone. I know people in Moscow and Bulgaria. I know people around the world."

His father, David, adds, "That fraternity he's part of, when he goes to Michigan and gets a business degree and maybe goes out, and maybe he never wrestles another day in his life, but he'll run into a guy who wrestled during the same period of time he did, and that camaraderie will always be there."

Sean Harrington says, "When you meet another wrestler that you don't know, say you're on a trip, it's like you hear about people who own Corvettes, you always wave to each other. It's the same thing with wrestling. You have a camaraderie there because you know what the other guy's been through."

"It's just focusing the energy for the match," says Ken Bigley. "When we're on the mat, we want to just beat the piss out of each other, but when we're off the mat we know what each other's going through because we've been there. As much as you focus on beating your opponent up, as much as you're enemies on the mat, as hard as you're going to hit him, once you're off the mat we're not violent people, we just like a violent sport."

Nick Feldman calls it "elegant violence."

During the matches, wrestlers lie around on the edges of the mats and watch. Wearing baggy sweats. They stay together, arms around each other, or locked in practice holds, in the kind of laid-back closeness you see only in men's fashion advertising anymore. Abercrombie & Fitch or Tommy Hilfiger magazine ads. Nobody seems to need "personal space." Nobody throws off "attitude."

"You're brothers," says Justin Petersen, who at seventeen has a 4.0 GPA and runs his own Internet marketing business. "We eat together. When you have lunch, it's with the other wrestlers, and all you do is talk about how hungry you are and you can't wait until after that weigh-in so you can eat this or that. How many tenths of a pound you're going to lose in a day."

Nick Feldman says, "As a whole, wrestlers are more comfortable with themselves. There's not too many egos getting blown everywhere because that's just all smoke. It's anti-NBA, pretty much."

"Hell," says Sara Levin. "Going through hell together does it. You know that a guy in Russia is going through the same thing that this guy here is, trying to cut this much weight. They've got to do the same thing to get on the mat. There's a bond in that we're not a glamorous sport. We're not high-profile, money. You know that you're down and dirty."

Like brothers, they even look alike. Many with broken noses. Cauliflower ears. Most have a kind of pulpy, boiled look from sweating hard and landing on their faces. They're all muscled like an anatomy chart. Most seem to have heavy brows.

"In our wrestling room, we usually have the heat high," says Mike Engelmann, whose long eyelashes are in contrast to his brow. "What that does is it kind of flushes your body. You sweat all of it out. You drink more and sweat it out again, and it kind of sinks the cheeks and the eyes in, a little bit, and the forehead's all you've got left sticking out there. I kind of like the look, because it shows you're working hard."

This brotherhood thing seems to end when the ref blows his whistle.

On Saturday, despite all the years of preparation, the freestyle tournament is all over, fast.

Joe Calavitta loses and is out of the Olympics.

In Junior competition, Justin Petersen wins, and as soon as he's off the mat he throws up.

The few people in the stands cheer, Sheldon Kim's wife, Sasha, saying softly, over and over, "Go, Shel. Go, Shel. Go, Shel . . ."

"When you're in there, one-on-one with somebody," says Timothy O'Rourke, "you can't even hear what's going on in the stands."

O'Rourke is pinned in five seconds.

Sheldon Kim loses.

Trevor Lewis wins his first match, but loses his second.

Chris Rodrigues wins his first match.

Sheldon Kim's younger brother, Sean, loses to Rodrigues.

Mark Strickland goes against Sean Harrington, with Lee Pritts coaching from a corner. Behind in the match, Strickland calls a time-out, screaming at Pritts, "I'm going to break his ribs!" His face twisted as if he's already crying.

"The toughest guys I know cry after matches because they put so much into it," Joe Calavitta says.

Lee Pritts says, "You become so close with a workout partner that they're like your own blood, and if they go out and lose a match, lose a *big* match, then you've just had your heart torn out."

Strickland loses to Harrington.

"I hate to see him lose," Pritts says. "I've seen him have so much success, that when he loses, it's crushing."

Pritts wins his match.

Chris Rodrigues wins his second match.

Ken Bigley wins his first and second matches, but loses his third.

Rodrigues loses his third match and is out of the freestyle tournament.

Sean Harrington and Lee Pritts are going to the Olympic finals in Dallas.

A medic refuses to say how many muscles are pulled, bones broken, joints dislocated. All that's, he says, "highly confidential."

And the freestyle tournament is over for another four years.

That night, in a tavern, a wrestler who didn't win talks about how he was screwed over by the ref in favor of a local hero, and how USA Wrestling should import impartial refs from other areas. This wrestler talks about going to Japan to earn $20,000 in an "ultimate fighting" match, then using the money to create a joint marketing venture between topless clubs and amateur fighting events.

"Many of these guys do the ultimate fighting because it's good money," says Sara Levin. "We have Olympians who are doing it. Kevin Jackson's done it. Half of our Greco Olympic team from '96 does it. I'm not thrilled that it's the professional outlet that our guys have, but it's their only option."

The wrestler in the tavern says he can sneak the money back from Japan and not pay any taxes. He plans to avoid state laws about professional fighting by paying fighters under the table. He signs autographs for little boys. He's huge and nobody disagrees with anything he says. And he talks and talks.

The next morning, Sunday, a Marine recruiting Humvee is parked outside the Young Arena, blaring heavy-metal rock music from giant speakers as two recruiters in Marine fatigues stand nearby.

Inside the arena, the mats are laid on top of each other, double-thick, in preparation for the Greco-Roman tournament.

"A lot of people are scared of Greco," says Michael Jones. "It took me a lot of years to get into it, because I was scared of it. Because of the throws. You got some serious throws."

Phil Lanzatella suits up to wrestle, the scar from his open-heart surgery running down the center of his chest. He explains how at least the third and final heart valve tear probably happened while he was practicing Greco-Roman wrestling with Jeff Green at the Olympic Training Center in 1997.

"I weighed about two-seventy and Green's probably about two-sixty, so we totaled about five-thirty, coming through the air at I don't know how many miles an hour. Twisting and turning. And we got next to some smaller guys. That space was tight. And they put their hands and feet up," he says. "And we came out of the turn and through the air, and I landed right on the guy's foot."

Lanzatella says, "I felt it. I knew what had happened, but I didn't think much of it. I'd taken worse shots than that."

Today, there's some talk about the darker side of wrestling, how someone snuck a camera into the weigh-ins at the Midlands tournament a few years ago and the best wrestlers in the world ended up naked on the Internet. People talk about how amateur wrestlers have been stalked by obsessed fans. Called late at night. Harassed. Killed.

"I know there was a lot of talk," says Butch Wingett. "DuPont was hot for Dave Schultz for a long time."

Former college wrestler Joe Valente says, "This sport gets so much disrespect. People think it's a bunch of homo men trying to feel each other up."

As the Greco competition starts, there's no one in the stands.

Keith Wilson wins his first match, loses his second, but will still go to the Olympic finals because he's already qualified in the Nationals.

Chris Rodrigues wins a single match and will go to the Olympic finals as a Greco-Roman wrestler. The only high school student to qualify.

With his father after the match, he says, "This is just great. I'm still in high school. I get to go back home and tell all my friends I'm going to the Olympic trials in Dallas."

Phil Lanzatella wins his first match three-zero.

His second match, Phil ties zero-zero in the first period, then loses a point to his opponent in the second period and loses the match in overtime.

Already the crowd of wrestlers is thin. People are getting out, catching planes. Tomorrow is Monday and everybody has to be back at work. Sean Harrington as a painting contractor. Tyrone Davis as a water-plant operator for the town of Hempstead, New York. Phil Lanzatella as a spokesman for the company who installed his heart valve and as an advertising account rep for Time Warner.

Lanzatella sits at the far side of the tournament floor while the last consolation matches wrap up. His wrestling shoes sit a few feet away.

"I got what I deserved," he says. "I haven't been training hard enough. I have different priorities now. My wife. My kids. A job."

He says, "Last time these shoes will see action."

He says, "Maybe I'll take up golf or something."

Sheldon Kim says, "This is probably it for me. I have other priorities. I have my little girl. After this, that's it for me. I've gotten enough out of the sport to know what I've accomplished."

Wrestlers leaving "the family" to concentrate on their own. Now almost no one is here at the Young Arena.

"Wrestling has a kind of cult following," says William R. Groves, who's driving back to Ohio State University tonight, to finish the last year on his Ph.D. in physics. "Your friends come. Your family comes. And I think a lot of people view wrestling as a boring sport."

Justin Petersen says, "It is a dying sport. I've heard some people say that boxing's a little bit worse, but wrestling's right there behind it. There's a lot of colleges dropping their wrestling programs. The high school popularity is going down. It doesn't have a lot of years left, that's what people say."

"It's dying at the collegiate level most of all," says Sean Harrington. "But I've read that at the kid level, the young children, it's more popular than ever. There's just lots of kids getting involved in wrestling because parents know what it can be to their children."

He says, "It's a hundred percent Title IX."

In the twenty-five years since the federal law that requires colleges to offer equal sports opportunities for men and women, more than 462 schools have dropped their wrestling programs.

"Title IX, that's a major factor," says Mike Engelmann. "All those colleges are getting screwed out of their wrestling programs because we have to have an equal amount of sports. I don't want to sound like a sexist or anything, but I really don't believe in it."

Even Olympic champion Kevin Jackson says, "I have a son, and he's started to wrestle a little bit, but he does tae kwon do, soccer, basketball, and I really hesitate to push him toward wrestling in any way because it is such hard work for little reward."

Still sitting near his shoes in the almost empty arena, Phil Lanzatella talks about his children, "More to the point, I'd push them to tennis or golf. Something noncontact, with lots of money."

Jackson says, "So many people around the country have wrestled, or they know someone who wrestled. They have some connection to it. We just have to do a better job of promoting our athletes so folks watching TV can make that connection."

"These guys," Engelmann says, "I'm sure all their kids are going to wrestle, too. And that's why it's not going to die. I want to have kids, and I'm not going to push it on them, but I hope they're going to want to wrestle."

Phil Lanzatella has a plane to catch, too.

"Maybe all this energy can be funneled into monetary gains," he says. He's been approached about writing a book. "Now I have the time to reflect and certainly the stories. From 1979 through today. I've been through about every aspect. Running for state legislator . . . going out with Mondale's daughter when we boycotted the Olympics in '80 . . . being a part of five Olympic teams—that's never been done before. Yeah, there's a lot."

He picks up his shoes and says, "I still have to call my wife . . ."

"It feels so good when you stop," says high school wrestling coach Steve Knipp. "It's such a demanding thing when you're doing it that when you stop cutting weight and get to eat, you never appreciated food so much in your life. Or when you get to just sit down, you never appreciated that chair so much. Or when you get to take a drink of water, you never appreciated water so much."

And now Lanzatella, Harrington, Lewis, Kim, Rodrigues,

Jackson, Petersen, all those ears. Davis, Wilson, Bigley, all those stalactite cauliflower ears are diffused out into the big world, where they'll blend in. Into jobs. Into families.

Where they'll only ever be noticed by other wrestlers.

Keith Wilson says, "It's a small family, but everybody knows each other."

And maybe amateur wrestling is dying, but maybe not.

At the Olympic team finals in Dallas, there are 50,170 paying spectators, and big-money corporate sponsors including Bank of America, AT&T, Chevrolet, and Budweiser.

In Dallas, one wrestler asks to perform an old ritual to mark the last match of his career. In this tradition, the wrestler puts his shoes in the center of the mat and covers them with a handkerchief. With the crowd silent, the wrestler kisses the mat and leaves his shoes behind.

Sean Harrington says, "I got a friend who used to tell me, 'If I wrestled, I'd be the best. I know I'd be the best. I know I could.' But he didn't. He didn't do it. So he could always just *think* that he could've been the best, but he never actually put on the shoes and went out and did it."

He says, "Just the fact that you've accomplished, and you've set your goals and you went after them, and you never were a 'woulda, shoulda, coulda.' You actually did it."

No one mentioned in this article made the Olympic team.

{You Are Here}

In the ballroom at the Airport Sheraton Hotel, a team of men and women sit inside separate booths, curtained off from each other. They each sit at a small table, the curtains enclosing a space just big enough for the table and two chairs. And they listen. All day, they sit and listen.

Outside the ballroom, a crowd waits in the lobby, writers holding book manuscripts or movie screenplays. An organizer guards the ballroom doors, checking a list of names on a clipboard. She calls your name, and you step forward and follow her into the ballroom. The organizer parts a curtain. You take a seat at the little table. And you start to talk.

As a writer, you have seven minutes. Some places you might get eight or even ten minutes, but then the organizer will return to replace you with another writer. For this window of time, you've paid between twenty and fifty dollars to pitch your story to a book agent or a publisher or movie producer.

And all day, the ballroom at the Airport Sheraton is buzzing with talk. Most of the writers here are old—creepy old, retired people clutching their one good story. Shaking their manuscript in both spotted hands and saying, "Here! Read my incest story!"

A big segment of the storytelling is about personal suffering. There's the stink of catharsis. Of melodrama and memoir. A writer friend refers to this school as "the-sun-is-shining-the-birds-are-singing-and-my-father-is-on-top-of-me-again" literature.

In the lobby outside the hotel ballroom, writers wait, practicing their one big story on each other. A wartime submarine battle, or being knocked around by a drunk spouse. The story about how they suffered, but survived to win. Challenge and triumph. They time each other with wristwatches. In just minutes, they'll have to tell their story, *and* prove how it would be perfect for Julia Roberts. Or Harrison Ford. Or, if not Harrison, then Mel Gibson. And if not Julia, then Meryl.

Then, sorry, your seven minutes is up.

The conference organizer always interrupts at the best part of the pitch, where you're deep into telling about your drug addiction. Your gang rape. Your drunken dive into a shallow pool on the Yakima River. And how it would make a great feature film. And, if not that, then a great cable film. Or a great made-for-television movie.

Then, sorry, your seven minutes is up.

The crowd out in the lobby, each writer holding his story in his hand, it's a little like the crowd here last week for the *Antiques Road Show*. Each person carrying some burden: a gilded clock or a scar from a house fire or the story of being a married, gay Mormon. This is something they've lugged around their whole life, and now they're here to see what it will fetch on the open market. Just what is this worth? This china teapot, or crippling spinal disease. Is it a treasure or just more junk.

Then, sorry, your seven minutes is up.

In the hotel ballroom, in those curtained cubicles, one person sits passive while the other exhausts himself. In that way, it's like a brothel. The passive listener paid to receive. The active speaker paying to be heard. To leave behind some trace of himself—always hoping this trace is enough to take root and grow into something bigger. A book. A baby. An heir to his story, to carry his name into the future. But the listener, he's heard it all. He's polite, but bored. Hard to impress. This is your seven minutes in the saddle—so to speak—but your whore is looking at his own wristwatch, wondering what's for lunch, planning on how to spend the stipend money. Then . . .

Sorry, your seven minutes is up.

Here's your life story, but reduced to two hours. What was your birth, your mother going into labor in the backseat of a taxi—that's now your opening sequence. Losing your virginity is the climax of your first act. Addiction to painkillers is your second-act build. The results of your biopsy is your third-act reveal. Lauren Bacall would be perfect as your grandmother. William H. Macy as your father. Directed by Peter Jackson or Roman Polanski.

This is your life, but processed. Hammered into the mold of a good screenplay. Interpreted according to the model of a successful box-office hit. It's no surprise you've started seeing every day in terms of another plot point. Music becomes your soundtrack. Clothing becomes costume. Conversation, dialogue. Our technology for telling stories becomes our language for remembering our lives. For understanding ourselves. Our framework for perceiving the world.

We see our lives in terms of storytelling conventions. Our serial marriages become sequels. Our childhood: our prequel. Our children: spin-offs.

Just consider how fast everyday people started using phrases like "fade to black." Or "wipe dissolve." Or fast-forward. Jump cut to . . . Flash back to . . . Dream sequence . . . Roll credits . . .

Then, sorry, your seven minutes is up.

It's twenty, thirty, fifty dollars for another seven minutes. For another shot at connecting with the bigger world. For selling your story. To turn that misery into big money. Book-advance money, or movie-option money. That big mega-jackpot.

A few years ago, only a few of these conventions shipped industry players from New York and Los Angeles, put them up in hotels, and paid them a stipend to sit here and listen. Now there are so many conventions that organizers must scrape the barrel a little, looking for any producer's assistant or associate editor who can spare a weekend to fly out to Kansas City or Bellingham or Nashville.

This is the Midwest Writers Conference. Or the Writers of Southern California Conference. Or the Georgia State Writers Conference. As a hopeful writer, you've paid to get in the door, for a name badge and a keynote lunch. There are classes to attend, lectures about technique and marketing. There's the mixed comfort and competition of other writers. Fellow writers. So many of them with a manuscript under one arm. You pay the extra money, the seven-minute money, to buy the ear of an industry player. To buy the chance to sell, and maybe you'll walk away with some money and recognition for your story. An experiential lottery ticket. A chance to turn lemons—a miscarriage, a drunk driver, a grizzly bear—into lemonade.

Straw, but spun into gold. Here in the big storytelling casino.

Then, sorry, your seven minutes is up.

In another way, this hotel ballroom, it's filled with people telling about their one awful crime. Spilling their guts about how they aborted a child. How they smuggled drugs stuffed up their ass all the way from Pakistan. Here's how they fell out of grace, the opposite of a hero's story. Here's how they can sell even their bad example—how it can help others. Prevent similar disasters. These people are here to find redemption. To them, each curtained booth becomes a confessional. Each movie producer, a priest.

It's no longer God waiting in judgment. It's the marketplace.

Maybe a book contract is the new halo. Our new reward for surviving with strength and character. Instead of heaven, we get money and media attention.

Maybe a movie starring Julia Roberts, bigger than life and pretty as an angel, is the only afterlife we get.

And that's only if . . . your life, your story is something you can package and market and sell.

In another way, this is so much like the crowd here last month, when a television game show was auditioning contestants. To answer brain teasers. Or the month before, when producers for a daytime talk show were here, looking for troubled people who wanted to air their problems on national television . . . fathers and sons who've shared the same sex partner. Or mothers suing for child support. Or anyone getting a sex change.

Then, sorry, your seven minutes is up.

The philosopher Martin Heidegger pointed out how human beings tend to look at the world as a standing stock of material, ready for us to use. As inventory to be processed into something more valuable. Trees into wood. Animals into meat. He called this world of raw natural resources: *bestand.* It seems inevitable that people without access to natural *bestand* such as oil wells or diamond mines, that they'd turn to the only inventory they do have—their lives.

More and more, the *bestand* of our era is our own intellectual property. Our ideas. Our life stories. Our experience.

What people used to endure or enjoy—all those plot-point events of potty training and honeymoons and lung cancer—now they can be shaped to best effect and sold.

The trick is to pay attention. Take notes.

The problem with seeing the world as *bestand*, Heidegger said, was it leads you to use things, enslave and exploit things and people, for your own benefit.

With this in mind, is it possible to enslave yourself?

Martin Heidegger also points out that an event is shaped by the presence of the observer. A tree falling in the forest is somehow different if someone is there, noting and accenting the details in order to turn it into a Julia Roberts vehicle.

If only by distorting events, tweaking them for more dramatic impact, exaggerating them to the point you forget your actual history—you *forget who you are*—is it possible to exploit your own life for the sake of a marketable story?

But then, sorry, but your seven minutes is up.

Maybe we should've seen this coming.

In the 1960s and '70s, televised cooking shows coaxed a rising class of people to spend their extra time and money on food and wine. From eating, they moved on to cooking. Led by how-to experts like Julia Child and Graham Kerr, we exploded the market for Viking ranges and copper cookware. In the

1980s, with the freedom of VCRs and CD players, entertainment moved in to become our new obsession.

Movies became the field where people could meet and debate, like they did over soufflés and wine a decade before. Like Julia Child had, Gene Siskel and Roger Ebert appeared on television and taught us how to split hairs. Entertainment became the next place to invest our extra time and money.

Instead of the vintage and bouquet and legs of a wine, we talked about the effective use of voice-over and backstory and character development.

In the 1990s, we turned to books. And instead of Roger Ebert it was Oprah Winfrey.

Still, the really big difference was, you could cook at home. You really couldn't make a movie, not at home. But, you could write a book. Or a screenplay. And those do become movies.

The screenwriter Andrew Kevin Walker once said that no one in Los Angeles is ever more than fifty feet from a screenplay. They're stowed in the trunks of cars. In desk drawers at work. In laptop computers. Always ready to be pitched. A winning lottery ticket looking for its jackpot. An uncashed paycheck.

For the first time in history, five factors have aligned to bring about this explosion in storytelling. In no particular order the factors are:

Free time.

Technology.

Material.

Education.

And disgust.

The first seems simple. More people have more free time. People are retiring and living longer. Our standard of living and social safety net allows people to work fewer hours. Plus, as more people recognize the value of storytelling—but strictly as book and movie material—more people see writing, reading, and research as something more than just a highbrow recreation. Writing's not just a nice little hobby. It's becoming a bona fide financial endeavor worth your time and energy. Telling anyone that you write always prompts the question "What have you published?" Our expectation is: writing equals money. Or good writing *should*. Still, it would be damn near impossible to get your work seen if not for the second factor:

Technology. For a small investment, you can be published on the Internet, accessible to millions of people worldwide. Printers and small presses can provide any number of on-demand hard-copy books for anybody with the money to self-publish. Or subsidy publish. Or vanity publish. Or whatever you want to call it. Anybody who can use a photocopy machine and a stapler can publish a book. It's never been so easy. Never in history have so many books hit the market each year. All of them filled with the third factor:

Material. As more people grow old, with the experience of a lifetime to remember, the more they worry about losing it. All those memories. Their best formulas, stories, routines for making a dinner table burst into laughter. Their legacy. Their life. Just a touch of Alzheimer's disease, and it could all disappear. Besides, all our best adventures seem to be behind us. So it feels good to relive them, to share them on paper. Organizing and making all that flotsam and jetsam make sense. Wrapping it up, neat and tidy, and putting a nice bow on top. The first volume in the three-volume boxed set that will be your life. The "best of" NFL highlights tape of your life. All in one place, your reasons for doing what you did. Your explanation why, in case anyone wants to know.

And thank God for factor number four:

Education. Because at least we all know how to keyboard. We know where to put the commas . . . kind of. Pretty much. We have automatic spell-checking. We're not afraid to sit down and take a swing at the job of book writing. Stephen King makes it look so easy. All those books. And Irvine Welsh, he makes it look like fun, the last place you can do drugs and commit crimes and not get arrested, or fat, or sick. Besides, we've read books all our lives. We've seen a million movies. In fact, that's part of our motivation, the fifth factor:

Disgust. Except for maybe six movies at the video store, the rest is crap. And most books, it's the same. Crap. We could do better. We know all the basic plots. It's all been broken down by Joseph Campbell. By John Gardner. By E. B. White. Instead of wasting more time and money on another crappy book or movie, how about you take a stab at doing the job? I mean, why not?

Then, sorry, your seven minutes is up.

Okay, okay, so maybe we're headed down a road toward mindless, self-obsessed lives where every event is reduced to words and camera angles. Every moment imagined through the lens of a cinematographer. Every funny or sad remark scribbled down for sale at the first opportunity.

A world Socrates couldn't imagine, where people would examine their lives, but only in terms of movie and paperback potential.

Where a story no longer follows as the result of an experience.

Now the experience happens in order to generate a story.

Sort of like when you suggest: "Let's not but *say* we did."

The story—the product you can sell—becomes more important than the actual event.

One danger is, we might hurry through life, enduring event

after event, in order to build our list of experiences. Our stock of stories. And our hunger for stories might reduce our awareness of the actual experience. In the way we shut down after watching too many action-adventure movies. Our body chemistry can't tolerate the stimulation. Or we unconsciously defend ourselves by pretending not to be present, by acting as a detached "witness" or reporter to our own life. And by doing that, never feeling an emotion or really participating. Always weighing what the story will be worth in cold cash.

Another danger is this rush through events might give us a false understanding of our own ability. If events occur to challenge and test us and we experience them only as a story to be recorded and sold, then have we lived? Have we matured? Or will we die feeling vaguely cheated and shortchanged by our storytelling vocation?

Already we've seen people use "research" as their defense for committing crimes. Winona Ryder shoplifting in preparation to play a character who steals. Pete Townsend visiting Internet kiddie-porn websites in order to write about his own childhood abuse.

Already our freedom of speech is headed for a collision with every other law. How can you write about a sadistic rapist "character" if you've never raped anybody? How can we create exciting, edgy books and movies if we only live boring, sedate lives?

The laws that forbid you to drive on the sidewalk, to feel the thud of people crumbling off the hood of your car, the crash of bodies shattering your windshield, those laws are *economically oppressive*. When you really think about it, restricting your access to heroin and snuff movies is a *restriction of your free trade*. It's impossible to write books, authentic books, about slavery if the government makes owning slaves illegal.

Anything "based on a true story" is more salable than fiction.

But, then, sorry, your seven minutes is up.

Of course, it's not all bad news.

There's the talk-therapy aspect to most writers' workshops.

There's the idea of fiction as a safe laboratory for exploring ourselves and our world. For experimenting with a persona or character and social organization, trying on costumes and running a social model until it breaks down.

There is all that.

One positive aspect is, maybe this awareness and recording will lead us to live more interesting lives. Maybe we'll be less likely to make the same mistakes again and again. Marry another drunk. Get pregnant, again. Because by now we know this would make a boring, unsympathetic character. A female lead Julia Roberts would never play. Instead of modeling our lives after brave, smart fictional characters—maybe we'll lead brave, smart lives to base our own fictional characters on.

Controlling the story of your past—recording and exhausting it—that skill might allow us to move into the future and write that story. Instead of letting life just *happen*, we could outline our own personal plot. We'll learn the craft we'll need to accept that responsibility. We'll develop our ability to imagine in finer and finer detail. We can more exactly focus on what we want to accomplish, to attain, to become.

You want to be happy? You want to be at peace? You want to be healthy?

As any good writer would tell you: unpack "happy." What does it look like? How can you demonstrate happiness on the page—that vague, abstract concept. Show, don't tell. Show me "happiness."

In this way, learning to write means learning to look at

yourself and the world in extreme close-up. If nothing else, maybe learning how to write will force us to take a closer look at everything, to really see it—if only in order to reproduce it on a page.

Maybe with a little more effort and reflection, you can live the kind of life story a literary agent would want to read.

Or maybe . . . just maybe this whole process is our training wheels toward something bigger. If we can reflect and know our lives, we might stay awake and shape our futures. Our flood of books and movies—of plots and story arcs—they might be mankind's way to be aware of all our history. Our options. All the ways we've tried in the past to fix the world.

We have it all: the time, the technology, the experience, the education, and the disgust.

What if they made a movie about a war and nobody came?

If we're too lazy to learn *history* history, maybe we can learn plots. Maybe our sense of "been there, done that" will save us from declaring the next war. If war won't "play," then why bother? If war can't "find an audience." If we see that war "tanks" after the opening weekend, then no one will green-light another one. Not for a long, long time.

Then, finally, what if some writer comes up with an entirely new story? A new and compelling way to live, before . . .

Sorry, your seven minutes is up.

{Demolition}

They come over the hills, sacrifices on their way here to die.

Today is Friday, the thirteenth of June. Tonight the moon is full.

They come here covered in decorations. Painted pink and wearing huge pig snouts, their floppy pink pig ears towering against the blue sky. They come, done up with huge yellow bows made of painted plywood. They come, painted bright blue and costumed to look like giant sharks with dorsal fins. Or painted green and crowded with little space aliens standing around slant-eyed under a spinning silver radar dish and flashing colored strobe lights.

They come, painted black with ambulance light bars. Or painted with brown desert camouflage and hand-drawn cartoons of missiles roaring toward Arabs riding camels. They come trailing clouds of special-effects smoke. Shooting cannons made from pipe and blasting black-powder charges.

They come with names like *Beaver Patrol* and the *Viking* and *Mean Gang-Green*, from dryland wheat towns such as Mesa and Cheney and Sprague. Eighteen sacrifices total, they come here to die. To die and be reborn. To be destroyed and be saved and come back next year.

Tonight is about breaking things and then fixing them. About having the power of life and death.

They come for what's called the Lind Combine Demolition Derby.

The where is Lind, Washington. The town of Lind consists of 462 people in the dry hills of the eastern reaches of Washington State. The town centers around the Union Grain elevators, which run parallel to the Burlington Northern railroad tracks. The numbered streets—First, Second, and Third—also run parallel to the tracks. The streets that intersect with the tracks begin with N Street as you enter town from the west end. Then comes E Street. Then I Street. All in all the streets spell out N-E-I-L-S-O-N, the family name of the brothers James and Dugal, who plotted the town in 1888.

The main intersection at Second and I is lined with two-story commercial buildings. The biggest building downtown is the faded pink art deco Phillips Building, home of the Empire movie theater, closed for decades. The nicest one is the Whitman Bank Building, brick with the bank's name painted in gold on the windows. Next door is the Hometown Hair salon.

The landscape for a hundred miles in any direction is sagebrush and tumbleweed, except where the rolling hills are plowed to raise wheat. There, dust devils spin. Train tracks connect the tall grain elevators of farm towns such as Lind and Odessa and Kahlotus and Ritzville and Wilbur. At the north end of Lind tower the concrete ruins of the Milwaukee Road train trestle, dramatic as a Roman aqueduct.

There's no record of where the name Lind came from.

At the south end of town are, the rodeo grounds, where bleacher seats line three sides of a dirt arena and jackrabbits graze in a gravel parking lot, around the dented and rusting hulks of retired demolition-derby contestants.

The what are combines, the big, slow machines used to harvest wheat. Each combine consists of four wheels: two huge chest-high wheels in front and two smaller, knee-high, wheels in back. The front wheels drive the machine, pulling it along. The rear wheels steer. In a pinch—say, when somebody rips off your rear wheels—you can steer with your front ones. Those front drive wheels each have brakes. To turn right you just stop your right wheel and let the left keep going. To turn left you do the opposite.

The front of each combine is a wide, low scoop called a header. It looks a little like the blade on the front of a bulldozer, only wider, lower, and made of sheet metal. It scoops up the wheat. From the header the wheat is sieved and threshed and shot out into a truck. The driver sits up, six feet off the ground, near the engine. Size- and shapewise, it looks very much like a man riding a boxy steel elephant.

Here, your header is what you use to pop another guy's tires. Or rip off *his* header. Or mangle his drive belts. That's why, in years past, guys filled their header scoops with concrete or welded them with layers of battleship plating or cut them down so they were harder for other combines to hook.

But that's against the rules now. Lots of rules changed after

Frank Bren ran over his own father in 1999, broke his leg, and left one huge front wheel parked on top of him. Since then Mike Bren has walked with a limp.

This year Frank is driving number 16, a Gleaner CH painted bright yellow and flapping with American flags and a huge yellow-ribbon bow cut out of plywood. It's christened *American Spirit, the Yellow Ribbon*. "The adrenaline rush when you're out there, it's just great," Frank Bren says. "It's not quite as good as sex, but it's close. You just love that sound of crushing metal."

The rest of the year Bren drives a grain truck. Dryland wheat ranching means no irrigation and not a lot of money. In the 1980s town fathers were looking for a way to raise cash for Lind's one-hundredth birthday. According to Mark Schoesler, the driver of number 11, a 1965 Massey Super 92 combine painted green and christened the *Turtle*, "Bill Loomis of Loomis Truck and Tractor was the instigator. He gave guys old combines. He sold them cheap. Traded them. Just whatever kind of deal it took, he helped them. They did so incredibly well that they couldn't quit."

Now, for the fifteenth year, some three thousand people will show up and pay ten bucks apiece to watch Schoesler ram his combine into seventeen others, again and again, for four hours, until only one still runs.

The rules: your header must be at least 16 inches above the ground. You can carry only 5 gallons of gas, and your gas tank must be sheltered in the bulk tank used for wheat at the center of each combine. You can use up to 10 pieces of angle iron to reinforce your rig. You must remove any glass from the cab. You can't fill your tires with calcium or cement for better traction. You must be at least 18 years old and wear a helmet and a seat belt. Your combine must be at least 25 years old. You must pay a $50 entry fee.

The judges give each driver a red flag to fly while he's still in the derby. "You just pull your flag and you're done," says eighteen-year-old Jared Davis, driver of number 15, a McCormick 151. "If your combine breaks down and it's not running anymore and you just can't move, they give you a certain amount of time and you just pull your flag and you're done." On the back end of Davis's number 15 is a hand-drawn cartoon of a mouse flipping the bird. Number 15 is christened *Mickie Mouse*.

Davis says, "These are just normal people out there for the fun of it. Just everyday working people. You get frustrations out, and you get to crash shit."

Despite all the rules, you can still drink. Tipping back a can of Coors, Davis says, "If you can walk, you can drive."

In the grassy pit-crew area behind the rodeo arena, Mike Hardung is here for his third year, driving *Mean Gang-Green,* a 1973 John Deere 7700. "My wife worries about me doing this, but I do a lot of crazy things," Hardung says. "Like race lawn mowers—riding lawn mowers. It's a pretty big deal. It's the Northwest Lawnmower Racing Association. We get up to forty miles an hour on riding lawn mowers."

About combine demolition, sitting up that high and crashing a mountain of steel, Hardung says, "It's chaotic. You don't know where you're at. You've really got to watch the weak spots, like the rear end of the combine and the tires. Then just go for the gusto and nail 'em. I'm a hitter."

Pointing out the pulleys and belts that link the engine and the front axle, Hardung says, "You have to protect your drive system so somebody can't get in there. If I tear off a belt I'm done."

Some combines have hydrostatic drives, no gearshifts, he says. The harder you push the lever, the faster the rig goes. Other combines have manual transmissions. Those drivers swear by a clutch and gearshift. Some swear by not drinking before the event. Everyone has a different strategy.

"I go out there," Hardung says. "I scope it out. Attack the bad guys. Leave the littler guys alone—unless they attack me first."

He says, "You see tires pop out there. We hit so hard we tear the headers off the front of combines or the rear ends off. A couple years ago we tipped one over on its side."

To repair the damage between heats, Hardung and his pit crew for *Mean Gang-Green* have brought along extra parts and supplies. Combine rear ends. Axles. Tires. Wheels. Welders. Cranes. Grinders. And beer.

"If farming gets any worse," Hardung says, "I'm going to bring my *new* combines over."

When asked whom he's most worried about, Hardung points to a huge combine, painted blue with a dorsal fin rising out of the top. It has large white teeth and a stuffed dummy that's half eaten and hanging out of the mouth of the header. Painted on the front in big black letters is "Josh."

"I'll be watching out for *Jaws*," Hardung says. "He's big because he's a hillside combine, and he's got this extra iron inside. And cast wheels. He's tough."

Josh Knodel is a rookie driver, eighteen years old. Since he was fourteen he and his friend Matt Miller have been bringing and repairing *Jaws,* a John Deere 6602 combine, and their fathers have driven it for them. Their first and second years, they took home the top prize. Last year they stopped dead with a blown front tire and only three combines left to beat.

"There's not much you can do to protect the tire itself," Knodel says. "The main thing I need to be careful of is not to get pinned, not to get where a combine locks me in from behind so somebody can then just hammer at my tires. I've got to try to stay out and move or else I'll get held up."

He says, "First, I'm going to try to get everybody in the dirt. I'll hit them in the back tires, try to knock their wheels out. You get down in the dirt like that and you're not nearly as fast or agile. You lose a lot of control. You lose a tire altogether and your whole rear end is just pushing in the dirt. Sometimes your rims even get ripped off and your whole ass end will be dragging in the dirt.

"I'm mainly excited," Knodel says. "I've been wanting to do this forever. Today's the day. But I've got butterflies. Last night it was tough to go to sleep." He says, "I can't remember missing a derby. It's derby time around our house. We've always come to town for the rodeo and the combine derby. This is a dream come true, definitely, being able to drive tonight. There's $300 if you win your heat. If you get second place in your heat, $200. Third place, you get $100. But if you win the whole derby, it's $1,000. There's definitely some prize money.

"There's no insurance," Knodel adds. "We don't sign anything, which is amazing. You'd think the Lions Club would have us sign something saying that if somebody gets hurt they're not liable, but I didn't sign anything. All of us out here, we're here to have fun. We realize we're at our own risk."

The grandstands are filling up. A long string of cars and trucks is pulling into the gravel parking lot. A water truck is wetting down the dirt in the rodeo arena.

At the beginning of the derby, the combines enter the arena and park in two long rows. As they wait, the crowd stands. The

Lind rodeo queen for the third year running, Bethany Thompson, wearing red-white-and-blue sequins and holding an American flag, gallops on her horse faster and faster around the assembled combines. As Thompson gains speed, her flag snapping in the wind, the combine drivers stand with their right hands over their hearts, and the three thousand onlookers recite the Pledge of Allegiance. People visiting here from the city get slapped or punched in the back and yelled at for not taking off their hats.

The derby consists of four heats: the first is for drivers who have competed here before, the second is for rookies, the third is another for experienced drivers, and the fourth begins with a consolation round for all the losing combines that can still run. After the fight, the winners from the first three heats enter the arena, and everyone still moving—winners and losers—fights to the death.

After the pledge, a judge reads a tribute written by driver Casey Neilson and the crew of combine number 9, a 1972 McCormick International 503 with an ambulance light bar spinning red and blue lights on top. Neilson's good-luck charm is the Afro wig he always wears while driving. People call him Afro Man. He calls his combine *Rambulance*.

Over the loudspeaker you hear: "The crew of Odessa Trading Company would like to take a moment to thank the men and women of EMS and local volunteer fire departments for all their hard work and dedication. If it weren't for you, some of us would not be here."

All but seven combines leave the arena, and the first heat begins.

Over the loudspeaker, a judge says, "Lord, help us have a good show and a safe show tonight."

Right off the bat, Mark Schoesler, in the *Turtle*, loses a rear tire. *Mean Gang-Green* and *J&M Fabrication* butt headers. The *BC Machine*, the *Silver Bullet*, and *Beaver Patrol* throw dirt in the air, chasing one another in a circle. The engines roar, and you breathe in the exhaust. *Mean Gang-Green*'s rear tire gets popped. *J&M Fabrication*'s rear tire gets popped, and the driver, Justin Miller, looks to be in trouble, stuck in one place and ducking down, disappearing into the engine compartment of his combine. The *Silver Bullet* is stopped dead and declared out by a judge, and driver Mike Longmeier drops his red flag. *Beaver Patrol* has a rear wheel completely torn off, then its rear axle, but it keeps going, dragging itself through the dirt with just its front wheels. Then *Red Lightnin'* crushes *Beaver Patrol*'s rear end. The engine housing pops open on *Mean Gang-Green* and smoke pours out. *Red Lightnin*'s engine catches fire. *J&M Fabrication* comes back to life, Miller reappearing in the driver's seat. *Beaver Patrol* drags along in the dirt. *J&M* rips the rear end off the *Turtle*. The beer keg falls off *Mean Gang-Green*. The rear axle rips off the *Turtle*. And Miller is stopped dead again. The judges wave the *Turtle* out, and Schoesler drops his red flag. *J&M Fabrication* is out, *Beaver Patrol* is out, and *Mean Gang-Green* is the winner.

In the pit the crew swarms *J&M Fabrication*, hammering and grinding metal. Welding sparks fly. Flat tires get changed. *J&M*'s Miller, headed to the consolation round, says, "I don't care who wins as long as we can hit as hard as we can for as long as we can."

Describing the best way to hit, he says, "I use the brakes. On these combines there's a brake for each side, so if you lock one of them up, you can spin around and get that one end of the header going. It'll be going five, six times as fast as the combine, and when you hit somebody right on the corner, it does a lot of damage to their machine."

You swing your header, he says, like a windmill punch.

"It will blow that tire. It will break that wheel right off. That header can be traveling twenty, twenty-five miles an hour. It makes a boom. It'll lift the ass end of the combine right off the ground. The ass end, it'll be one, two feet off the ground."

Between heats a forklift and a tow truck enter the arena and clear away the dead—the busted angle iron and crushed headers. Rodeo queen Thompson throws T-shirts into the audience. The beer flows.

Back in the pit area, rookie drivers like Davis and Knodel, all of them college age except Garry Bittick, driving the *Tank,* line up for their heat.

Within the first minute, Jeff Yerbich and his *Devastating Deere* are dead, the result of two popped rear tires. *Little Green Men* rams the *Tank*, tilting the combine so high it almost topples over backward. *Jaws* loses a rear wheel. *Mickie Mouse* has its header crushed and wadded up like tinfoil. The *Tank* stops dead and drops its red flag. *Jaws* chases *Mickie Mouse* in a circle. Knodel drives his header into the *Mouse*'s front tires, popping them. With the *Mouse* stopped, *Jaws* keeps ramming it until the judges make the dead combine drop its flag. *Jaws* loses a rear tire but drags itself along. The *Viking* is dead. The *Tank* has its header ripped off. Time runs out, leaving *Jaws* and *Little Green Men* tied as the winners.

In the pit area Bittick is recovering from nearly toppling under the five tons of number 5, the *Tank.* At forty-seven years old, he's getting into the rookie game a little late. His son Cody was supposed to be home from the army to drive but had run out of leave time. Instead, Cody sent the flags—an Army 82nd Airborne flag, an MIA flag, and a U.S. Army flag—that fly on the International Harvester combine, the one painted with desert camouflage and cartoons of camel-riding Arabs being chased by cruise missiles.

"It was just a lot of hard hits, everybody hitting at one time, head-on," Bittick says. "Of course, the tail end of my machine came up and tipped my header off, and we broke down. We could have flipped over." He says, "It gets your heart pumping. Without a seat belt it'll kick you right out of there."

For first-timers Davis and Knodel, it was a carnival fun ride. "It was *great*! It was funner than hell," says Davis, holding a beer can in one hand while his crew preps *Mickie Mouse* for the consolation round. "I got to go out there and beat the shit out of people for fun."

For Knodel and *Jaws*, tying for first was a little more work. "It was way more than I expected," Knodel says. "I didn't think I was going to have to concentrate as hard as I did. I was sweating very hard up there."

One of the few drivers not drinking beer or vodka, Knodel describes how it feels to be high up in the middle of the dust and the cheering: "Actually, you don't hear anything. I couldn't hear the crowd. The only thing I could hear was my engine. My engine actually powered out on me. I was going, and I couldn't hear that my engine had stopped. With the adrenaline pumping, I was still looking for somebody to come get me. The only way I knew I had the engine fired back up was that I could look over and see the fan blades, and finally I saw them spinning again. Then I was ready to go."

In the third heat the combines start out parked with their rear ends together, facing outward like the spokes in a wheel. Among another set of experienced drivers, *Rambulance* slices a rear tire of *Good Ol' Boys*. *Porker Express* rips the rear end off *BC*

Machine. Good Ol' Boys crushes the rear end of *American Spirit,* shattering its rear axle. *Porker Express* loses its rear axle tie rods and steering. American Spirit digs itself too deep into the dirt and drops its flag, dead. *Porker Express* locks its header under the rear end of *Rambulance. BC Machine* is stopped, with its engine cover open and smoking; a moment later Chet Bauermeister gets it going again. *Porker Express* gets crushed between *Good Ol' Boys* and *BC Machine. Good Ol' Boys* loses both rear tires but keeps going on the rims. *BC Machine* is dead again. *Good Ol' Boys* rams *Porker Express* from behind, driving its pink rear end into the dirt. *Good Ol' Boys* gets to work, ramming *BC Machine. Porker Express* is dead. *Rambulance* is dead. *Good Ol' Boys* shoves *BC Machine* in circles until Bauermeister drops his flag. *Good Ol' Boys* driver Kyle Cordill is the winner.

In the pit area, winning and losing teams repair their combines for the final heat. The welding rods, cutting torches, and grinders shower sparks into the dry grass, and people chase the little wildfires, putting them out with cans of beer. Barbecues grill hot dogs and hamburgers. Kids and dogs roam around combines tilted and balanced on jacks.

Near number 17, *Little Green Men,* a group of girls drink beer and eye driver Kevin Cochrane.

Twenty years old, Cochrane says, "Yeah, there are combine-demolition groupies. I don't think there are groupies from Lind, but they're from other towns. They kind of follow the little circuit, I think. There are only two derbies, so that's a little circuit."

Cochrane looks at the girls as one of them leaves her friends and heads over. "What are the groupies like? First of all," he says, "she's kind of a hick. Cowboy boots and shit like that. Kind of just the country way, but not like her." He nods as the girl walks up. Her name is Megan Wills. When asked why there are no women drivers, she says, "Because it's fucked! Josh got his ass kicked!"

"There used to be women drivers," Cochrane says.

"One! A long time ago!" shouts Wills, whose brother is on the pit crew for number 14, *Beaver Patrol*. "There's no women driving because that shit's fucked-up! I'm not going to take my ass in there. Fuck that! I'd rather get drunk and service all the hotties than fuckin' drive that shit! Hell, no!"

Cochrane tilts back his beer, then says, "I think if you don't drink any, you get too nervous. You get in there and you're all nerved up and shit. You got to get a little laid-back."

Before the consolation round, the judges walk through the pit area, telling people their thirty minutes of repair time is more than up. Only *Mickie Mouse* and *J&M Fabrication* are ready and waiting in the arena. The sun is below the horizon, and it's getting dark fast. Over the loudspeaker the judges announce: "We need nine combines in the ring. We only have two. We got seven to go."

Frank Bren, the driver of *American Spirit*, runs up, his T-shirt and hands soaked dark with motor oil, sweat, and crusted blood. "We're not going to make it," he tells the judges. "We can't get a hydraulic line changed out."

A judge reads the names of the combines still expected in the arena. "You're pushing the time limit," he says. "And you're pushing the judges."

Rambulance enters the ring, dragging a flat rear tire. *Red Lightnin'* makes it in. The *Silver Bullet* limps in. As the round starts, *Red Lightnin'* rams *Rambulance,* and sparks fly from the hit. The *Silver Bullet* digs its header into the front tires of *J&M Fabrication.* *Rambulance* loses its rear axle. *Mickie Mouse* loses a rear wheel. *J&M Fabrication* rams head-on into *Red Lightnin'*. Then *Rambulance* butts headers with *J&M* so hard that the rear ends of both combines bounce three feet into the air. *Mickie Mouse* snags *Red Lightnin'* hard enough to rip both rear wheels off, then pops a front tire. The hit rips the header off *Mickie Mouse,* and Davis drops his flag. He sits, sprawled in the driver's seat, his arms spread and his face tipped up at the dark sky. *Rambulance* drags itself around a field littered with bolts and scraps of metal. The *Silver Bullet* and *J&M Fabrication* slam *Red Lightnin'* so hard that the hit kills the *Silver Bullet*. Then *J&M* drops its flag.

While we wait for the wreckers to clean up and the winners to enter for the final showdown, Thompson throws more T-shirts into the stands. A huge orange moon comes up and seems to stop, balanced on the horizon.

The winners from the first three heats and any surviving combines enter the arena. It's full dark, and the red flags next to each driver look black, outlined against the smoke and dust. The radiator is failing on *BC Machine,* and the little Massey 510 combine is lost in a cloud of white steam. The engines of all nine combines roar together, and the final heat begins.

Right away *Little Green Men* loses its rear end and sits dead in a corner. *Jaws* rams the rear end of *Beaver Patrol*, killing it on the spot. *BC Machine* darts around the ring, filling the arena with steam from its spouting radiator. As a Burlington Northern freight train speeds past, blowing its whistle above the demolition noise, *Jaws* finds itself stuck, its header hooked under the dead rear end of *Beaver Patrol*. *Porker Express* crushes the ass end of *Mean Gang-Green*. The *Turtle* hides out, sitting with its rear wheels braced against the edge of the ring, where no combine can hit it without forcing it into the packed crowd. The *Porker Express* stops, dead. The *Turtle* ventures out to hit *Rambulance*, which now has no rear axle. In a corner *Little Green Men* sits dead, Cochrane's silver radar dish still spinning.

Hiding out at the edge, number 11, the *Turtle,* isn't a crowd favorite. "Some say I'm a sandbagger," says Schoesler, its driver. "That I just avoid contact a little too much. I like to think of it as the old Muhammad Ali rope-a-dope. Lay on the ropes and let them pound you where it doesn't hurt. And if there's an opening, you jab them and then retreat. It's worked pretty well over the years."

For Schoesler, who represents the Ninth Legislative District in the Washington State House of Representatives, the derby is a chance to campaign. He's planning to run for the State Senate.

"Being an elected official always generates a few jabs," he says. "All in fun, I hope. And a winner from a previous derby is a marked man. Having won in the past, I'm a target. Being an elected official makes me a double target."

In the arena now, *BC Machine* still fills the air with steam, and sparks shoot from its engine. The *Turtle* hides back, safe against the crowd of spectators.

Rambulance drops its flag. *Mean Gang-Green* rams the *Turtle,* driving it back into the crowd. *J&M Fabrication* rams the *Turtle,* and the dead combines sit, black and wrecked, just obstacles in the dark smoke- and steam-filled arena. The *Turtle* tries to escape and ends up pinched between *Good Ol' Boys, Mean Gang-Green,* and *J&M Fabrication. BC Machine* stops dead but with its radiator still steaming. The *Turtle* escapes, leaving its three attackers to slam one another. The header on *J&M* is still factory perfect, but the combine has no steering left in its ass end. You can smell hot, bitter brake fluid, and *J&M Fabrication* stops, with Miller stooped down, trying to restart the engine. The header drops off *Mean Gang-Green,* and Hardung is out. The *Turtle* still hides at the edge. *Good Ol' Boys* can hardly steer.

As the clock runs out, the judges rule. The money for first and second place is split between *Mean Gang-Green* and the *Turtle. Good Ol' Boys* takes third.

By 10:00 P.M. it's over, except for the serious drinking. Already cowboy boots kick up dust on their way to the parking lot. Country music mixes with hip-hop, and the air turns pink from thousands of taillights and brake lights waiting to turn onto the highway.

Terry Harding and the team for *Red Lightnin'* say, "Find us come midnight or one o'clock and we'll be blitzed."

Kevin Cochrane will go back to studying agriculture at Washington State.

Frank Bren will go back to driving his grain truck.

Mark Schoesler will no doubt go back to state government for another term. And the combines—*Red Lightnin'*, *Jaws*, *Beaver Patrol*, *Orange Crush*—will sit parked and rusting until it's time to fix them and crash them and fix them and crash them, again and again, next year.

This is the way the men of Adams County come back together. The farmers, now working at jobs in the city. The families spreading apart. The kids, whose shared years in high school get further and further behind them. This is their structure of rules and tasks. A way to work and play, together. To suffer and celebrate. To reunite.

Until next year, it's all over. Except for tomorrow's parade. The rodeo and the barbecue. The stories and the bruises.

"They'll all be walking stiff tomorrow," says derby organizer Carol Kelly. "They'll have sore shoulders and arms. And their necks, they'll barely be able to turn their heads."

She says, "Of course they get hurt. If they tell you otherwise, they're lying so you think they're tough."

{My Life as a Dog}

The faces that make eye contact, they're twisted into sneers.
The top lip pulled up to show teeth, the whole face bunched
around the nose and eyes. One blond Huck Finn kid walks
along after us, slapping our legs and shouting, "I can see your
NECK! Hey, asshole! I can see your neck from behind . . ."

A man turns to a woman and says, "Christ, only in
Seattle . . ."

Another middle-aged man says, loud, "This town has gotten
way too liberal . . ."

A young man with a skateboard under one arm says, "You
think you're cute? Well, you're not. You're just stupid. You
look fucking stupid . . ."

This wasn't about looking good.

As a white man, you can live your whole life never not fitting in. You never walk into a jewelry store that sees only your black skin. You never walk into a bar that sees only your boobs. To be Whitie is to be wallpaper. You don't draw attention, good or bad. Still, what would it be like, to live with attention? To just let people stare. To let them fill in the blank, and assume what they will. To let people project some aspect of themselves on you for a whole day.

The worst part of writing fiction is the fear of wasting your life behind a keyboard. The idea that, dying, you'll realize you only ever lived on paper. Your only adventures were make-believe, and while the world fought and kissed, you sat in some dark room, masturbating and making money.

So the idea was, a friend and I would rent costumes. Me, a spotted, smiling Dalmatian. Her, a brown dancing bear. Costumes without gender clues. Just fun-fur suits that hid our hands and feet and big, heavy papier-mâché heads that kept anyone from seeing our faces. This gave people no visual clues, no facial expressions or gestures to decode—just a dog and a bear walking around, shopping, being tourists in downtown Seattle.

Some of this I knew to expect. Every December, the international Cacophony Society hosts a party called "Santa Rampage" where hundreds of people come into a city, all of them dressed as Santa Claus. No one is black or white. No one is young or old. Male or female. Together they become a sea of red velvet and white beards storming the downtown, drinking and singing and driving the police nuts.

At a recent Santa Rampage, police detectives met an arriving planeload of Santa Clauses at the Portland airport, corralling them with guns and hot pepper spray and announcing, "Whatever you're planning, the city of Portland, Oregon, will not look upon it kindly if you burn Santa Claus in effigy . . ."

Still, five hundred Santas has a power that a lonely bear and dog do not. In the lobby of the Seattle Art Museum they sell us tickets for fourteen bucks. They talk to us about the exhibits, the portraits of George Washington on loan from the nation's capital. They tell us where to find the elevators and give us museum maps, but the moment we push the elevator button—they throw us out. No refund for the tickets. No slack. Just a lot of sad head shaking and a brand-new security policy that bears and dogs may buy tickets but they may not look at the art.

A block away from the museum doors, the guards still follow us, until a new group of guards from the next building has us under surveillance. Another block down Third Avenue, a Seattle Police car cruises up, following us at a creep as we head north to the retail shopping center.

In the Pike Place Market, young men wait for the dog to walk past, then throw punches or karate kicks into the black-spotted fur. Right in the kidneys. Into the back of my elbows or knees, hard. Every time, every kick and fist. Then, these same men, they jump back, rolling their eyes at the ceiling and pretending to whistle as if nothing has happened.

These people behind mirrored sunglasses, dressed alike behind the stiff attitude of hip-hop and skateboards, being young downtown and looking to fit in. Outside the Bon Marché, along Pine Street, young men throw rocks, denting the papier-mâché heads and pounding the fur. Young women run up in groups of four or five, holding digital cameras the size of silver cigarette packs and clutching the dog and bear as photo props. Squeezed in, smiling with their breasts pressing warm and their arms around an animal neck.

The police still trailing us, we run inside the Westlake Center, running past Nine West on the first level of the shopping mall. Running past the Mill Stream store—"Gifts from the

Pacific Northwest"—we're running past Talbots and Mont Blanc, past Marquis Leather. People ahead of us pull back, standing tight against Starbucks and LensCrafters, creating a constant vacuum of empty white floor for us to run into. Behind us, walkie-talkies crackle and male voices say, ". . . suspects are in sight. One appears to be a dancing bear. The second suspect is wearing a large dog head . . ."

Kids scream. People pour out of the stores for a better look. Clerks come forward to stare, their faces peering from behind sweaters and wristwatches in display windows. It's the same excitement we felt as kids when a dog got into our grade school. We're running past Sam Goody, past the Fossil store, the walkie-talkies right behind us, the voices saying, ". . . the bear and the dog are westbound, headed down the first-level access way to the Underground Eatery . . ." We're running past Wild Tiger Pizza and Subway Sandwiches. Past teenage girls sitting on the floor, yakking on the pay phones. "Affirmative," the walkie-talkie voice says. From behind us, it says, ". . . I'm about to apprehend both alleged animals . . ."

All this fuss, this chase. Young men stone us. Young women grope us. Middle-aged men look away, shaking their heads and ignoring the dog that waits in line with them at Tully's for a grande latte. A middle-aged Seattle guy, tall with a blond ponytail and his pants rolled to his knee, exposing bare calves, he walks past, saying, "You know, there's a leash law in this town."

An older woman with her beauty parlor hair silver-rinsed and sprayed into a pile, she tugs at one spotted dog arm, tugging the fur and asking, "What are you promoting?" She trails along, still tugging the fur, asking, *"Who's paying you to do this?"* Asking louder, "Can't you hear me?" Saying, "Answer me." Asking, "Who do you work for?" Saying, "Tell me . . ." She's clutching us for half a block, until her grip breaks.

Another middle-aged woman, pushing a stroller the size of a grocery cart, packed with disposable diapers, formula, toys and clothes and shopping bags, with one tiny baby lost somewhere in the mix, in the concrete middle of Pike Place Market, this woman shouts, "Everyone get back! Get back! For all we know they could be strapped with bombs inside those costumes . . ."

Everywhere, there's the brain scramble as security guards create public policy to deal with people dressed as animals.

A friend of mine, Monica, used to work as a clown for hire. While she twisted balloons into animals at corporate parties, men were always offering her money to fuck. Looking back, she says that any woman who'd dress as a fool, who'd refuse to look attractive, she was seen as loose, wanton, and willing to fuck for money. Another friend, Steve, wears a wolf costume to Burning Man each year and fucks his brains out because, he says, people see him as less than human. Something wild.

By now, the backs of my knees hurt from taking kicks. My kidneys ache from getting punched, and my shoulder blades from pitched rocks. My hands are running with sweat. My feet are sore from too much walking on concrete. On Pine Street young women drive past, waving from cars and screaming, "We love you . . ."

All these people behind their own masks: their sunglasses and cars and fashions and haircuts. Young men drive past, screaming, "Goddamn fucking FAGS . . ."

By now, I don't give a shit. This dog could walk around this way forever. Walking taller. Blind and deaf to people's shit. I don't need to wave, to pander and pose with kids for pictures. I'm just a dog smoking a cigarette outside Pottery Barn. I lean back, one leg lifted against the facade of Tiffany and Company. I'm just the Dalmatian making a cell-phone call in front of Old Navy. It's the kind of cool, a feeling of being self-contained, that white guys can live a lifetime without.

By now it's sweating hot. It's late afternoon, and FAO Schwarz is almost deserted. Inside the big glass doors, a young guy is dressed as a toy soldier in a red tailcoat with a double row of brass buttons and a towering black helmet. The escalators are empty. The Barbie Shop is empty. The toy soldier plays with a radio-controlled race car, alone and trapped inside on the first sunny day Seattle has seen in months.

The toy soldier looks up from his job, at the dog and bear coming through the door, and he smiles. Ignoring his race car, letting it drive into a wall, the soldier says, "You guys rock!" He says, "You SO totally rule."

{Confessions in Stone}

When you're flying from Seattle to Portland, Oregon, as you turn to make your final approach into the airport from the east, there, outside the airplane windows, right below you . . . there it is:

A vision of white battlements and towers. Narrow white turrets and a drawbridge that spans a murky lake, its water pooling around a crumbling stone ruin. At one end, stands a massive round keep.

There, in the hills above the blue-collar town of Camas, Washington, where most days the air smells like the sour steam from the paper mill, there it is:

A castle.

A big castle. A real castle.

It's surrounded by little hobby farms and tract housing developments and the huge postmodern complex of the new Camas High School, but this is a Viking castle. Complete with racks filled with battle-axes, ready for the next fight. A fire-breathing dragon. Gates sixteen feet tall. All that and a Bunn coffeemaker. A Frigidaire refrigerator and Jerry Bjorklund, the builder and resident Viking.

Fly four hundred miles northeast, into the Selkirk Mountains on the Idaho panhandle, and you'll find a Bavarian-style castle perched in the snow fields at 4,600 feet. A fortress of stone and stained glass with a heated indoor swimming pool, double-fisted chunks of semiprecious yellow citrine, purple amethyst and pink-rose quartz embedded in the walls. Arches and pinnacles and spires, all of it hand-built, rock by rock, by a single man named Roger DeClements.

And somewhere between the Viking and the Bavarian is a tall narrow tower of four floors rising from a rocky point at the edge of the White Salmon River. In this third castle, a nude mannequin sits on the rail of a third-floor balcony, ready to distract the white-water rafters and kayakers who drift past and only glimpse her bare breasts for a minute before the river pulls them around the next bend and leaves them wondering what they saw. Or thought they saw: a cluster of gray stone towers. Heavy timber balconies. A waterfall trickling, green, down the front of a stone terrace. Massive canopy beds and antique armoires and an ex–jet fighter pilot named Bob Nippolt.

There, deep in the woods of the Cascade Mountains, it's a vision . . . a fantasy.

A castle.

"There seems to be this underground of castle people," says Roger DeClements, who changed his name from the very German family name Grimes. He says, "There must be between twenty and thirty people building castles in the United States right now. A lot of them are people doing do-it-yourself work, so they're going kind of slow. They're starting out like I did with their designs. But there's also a couple very rich folks who just—*boom*—go and build the biggest castle they can imagine."

Here a man's home is his castle. And vice versa. And maybe this trend is no more than a bigger version of the basic nesting instinct. What SUVs are to regular cars, these castles are to regular houses. Solid. Safe. Secure.

Or maybe castle building is a rite of passage. A form of meditation or reflection. During the second half of his life, after his mother died, the psychologist and philosopher Carl Jung set to work building a stone castle. He built it in Bollingen, on the shore of Lake Zurich in Switzerland. He called it his "confession in stone."

Or maybe castle building is a reaction to the fast-paced, short-lived spirit of our times. For architects, the modern era ended at 3:32 P.M. on July 15, 1972, when the Pruitt-Igoe housing development was dynamited in St. Louis, Missouri. It had been a prize-winning example of clean-line, boxy, International-style architecture. What architects called "a machine for living." By 1972, it was a failure. The residents hated the place, and the city declared it uninhabitable.

That same year, the architect Robert Venturi declared that most people's idea of utopia was closer to Disneyland or Las Vegas than to a modern glass-box apartment.

So whether building a castle is a statement or a mission, a nesting instinct or a penis extension . . . what follow are the stories of three men who each left a career—a policeman, a building contractor, and a jet pilot—and set out to build a castle. Here are the mistakes they made. And what they've learned along the way.

Walking through his castle, high on its granite mountain above Sandpoint, Idaho, Roger DeClements is forty-seven years old but looks twenty-seven, with long thick hair that hangs past his shoulders. He's got wiry arms and legs and wears a white, long-sleeved T-shirt and blue jeans. Tennis shoes. His fingernails are a surprise, long and ridged, maybe from the years when he played bass with a rock band.

"I've always been building," Roger says. "I built my first house in 1975. Then we rented a place and it was right next to the railroad tracks and people would always come knocking on the door. Then we saw the movie *The Beastmaster*, and that gave me some ideas. I thought a castle would be good because it would be secure. Then I also noticed houses were depreciating with time where a castle would appreciate with time and not rot away."

By now Roger's built three castles—from his first, which took five weeks, to his latest, which is for sale at a million-dollar price. "Basically, I thought it would be fun," he says. "Fun to live in. Fun for people to look at. And then the fact that it would be there permanently, and you could pass it on for generations."

For Jerry Bjorklund, it was fun plus a little alcohol.

"I'm a pretty good sipper," he says. "I'm drinking some Black Velvet one night, and I called a friend on the city council, and I said, 'I'm going to build a castle.' And he said, 'No, you can't do that.' And I said, 'Yeah, I am.' And the next morning I wake up and thought, 'Goddamn it. I told him I was going to build a castle, so here I go . . .'"

But why a castle?

Jerry shrugs and says, "I don't know. Nordic heritage or whatever. I always had an interest in them. And it seemed like a good idea. Nobody else had one."

With a dark tan from winters spent fishing in Mazatlán, Jerry sits in an apartment that occupies one wing of his castle in the green hills above Camas, Washington. He's fifty-nine years old, a retired officer of the Camas Police Department. His face is square with a heavy cleft chin and a Viking's bushy mustache gone gray. His heavy eyebrows and full head of hair are gray. He wears a black pocket T-shirt and jeans. On his forearms, old tattoos have turned dark blue.

Jerry smokes Delicados cigarettes from Mexico. "I bring them back," he says. "I get them for seven dollars a carton." And he laughs a rumbling smoker's laugh.

His light-blue eyes almost match the pale-blue countertops of the apartment's kitchen. He drinks black coffee and wears a watch with a heavy silver wristband.

His ancestors were Norwegian, and he was born in North Dakota but raised here in Washington State. He retired in 1980 and built a small A-frame house. In 1983, he started his dream castle.

"I was going to build it out of rock," Jerry says. "We had a lot of rock here. And I struggled with that for probably six months. Rocks. Mortar. Washing rocks. Jesus."

Digging rock out of a pit on his five and one-half acres, Jerry built a twenty-two-foot tower. He says, "I got part of a tower built, and I could see that this was going to be a real labor-intensive adventure."

He laughs and says, "And I thought, 'There has got to be a better way.' "

So he called his uncle, a master plasterer for fifty years, and asked about stucco. By July of 1983, he was building his castle out of wood and covering it with stucco.

He says, "It's a lot of two-by-sixes and a lot of half-inch plywood and a *lot* of staples."

The framing is two-by-sixes every two feet, covered with sheets of half-inch plywood. Stapled to the plywood is fifteen-pound tar paper, then stucco wire, which looks like chicken wire but is offset to allow the plaster to get behind the wire and harden around it. "They put the scratch coat on—that's the first coat," Jerry says. "Then you put the brown coat on. You smooth that out. Then I came back with an acoustic sprayer, like you'd use to spray acoustic ceilings, and we used white sand and Zonolite insulation. We'd mix this up in the acoustic machine and apply that with air pressure."

He says, "Just on the exterior alone, there's 380,000 pounds of sand and cement that I personally troweled on by hand. Then, I have a severe fear of heights, and it was a hell of a task when my last scaffold was up at thirty-two feet. Ah, Jesus, that was a terrible job, and it took me three days to do the parapet."

The castle consists of a three-story "keep" at the east end. Extending west from the keep, two wings enclose a central courtyard. The west end of the courtyard is enclosed by a garage. The keep is about 1,500 square feet, with 500 on each floor. Each of the wings is about 1,000 square feet with one wing finished as an apartment and the other as storage space. The garage is about 500 square feet.

Thinking about the construction, Jerry lights another cigarette. He laughs and says, "There are some fantastic stories."

To finish the forty-foot walls of the keep, Jerry built a tripod on the roof, using the tongues made to tow mobile homes—basically, ten-inch steel I beams with a length of well casing as a boom. He says, "This is really scary. I built a four-by-eight-foot basket. It was tall enough you could stand in it, and it was closed in with wire on three sides so you could actually work on the surface of the building. And I got this one-ton twelve-volt electric winch with five-sixteenths cable, and I got *that* mounted on the top of the cage with a remote control. Picture this: two guys get into this with a roll of wire or paper or whatever they're going to apply. We'd get in there and pull ourselves up to where we wanted to work. Well, I cut the well casing too short when I built it, so the basket wouldn't go outside enough to work on the parapet."

There, where the top of the tower flares out, just before the crenellated top, Jerry would have to trowel stucco while leaning backward over nothing but forty feet of air.

"You could work about halfway up the pitch-out, but it was a real son of a bitch after that point." He says, "We're up there dangling on this five-sixteenths-inch cable, and I had two people on the ground with ropes trying to steady this basket. The next day I went to town and bought a bunch of lumber, and we made scaffolding."

It took him four days just to assemble the scaffolding.

Getting the money together was even more tough.

"The goddamn bankers," Jerry says, "I talked to them one time while the castle was under construction, and they said there was no guarantee I was ever going to get it done—so I just said, 'To hell with it . . .'"

He adds, "You won't get a loan from a bank. I've had appraisers come out three different times. What they ultimately conclude is that it is a 'nonconforming structure.'" And he laughs. "That just fits it to a tee. Nonconforming . . . I love it.

"So I'd scratch up a few bucks, and do a little bit," he says. "Then I'd run out of money so I'd have to go back and do something else to make a few bucks. Then I'd come back and hit it again. You learn how to wire and plumb. You just learn as you go. I wouldn't say I'd never do it again. But thank God I'm getting too old."

The floors inside the keep are supported by eight-by-eight

vertical posts that hold eight-by-twelve beams, rough cut by a friend from the hearts of trees.

"The first two floors weren't too bad," Jerry says. "The third floor was a real son of a bitch. The height. Evergreen Truss brought their truss truck out, and he had to put the extension on his boom, and he could still just barely get up there and set those beams for me. It was goddamn scary."

The first-floor kitchen includes a 1923 wood-burning kitchen stove and a half bath. The living room is on the second floor. The bedroom and a full bathroom are on the top floor. "When you go to the toilet here," Jerry says, "you're thirty feet off the deck."

Divorced now, at the time he built the keep Jerry Bjorklund was married. "You get women involved and it's 'I've got to have this. And I've got to have that. I've got to have a dining room set over here, and I've got to have a dishwasher.'" Jerry says, "You start accommodating all that and it takes away from what I originally had in mind to do."

Once you're inside, the keep feels like a house, complete with wall-to-wall carpeting and crystal chandeliers. "It's like living any other place," he says. "You just forget about it."

When he started building, Jerry still didn't have anybody's official permission.

"At this point I was one-hundred-percent antigovernment," he says. "Of course I had no permits, no nothing, and my brother said, 'You'd better get some permission to do what you're doing.' So I built a scale model and took it down to the building department and said, 'This is what I want to build.' The old guy looked at it and said, 'How tall is it?' And I said it's going to be forty feet. And he said, 'No, you can't do forty feet. You can only go thirty-six, by code.'"

The reason was, traditionally, the longest ladder a fire engine carries is forty feet. So Jerry filed for a variance, showing how his top floor would only be thirty-six feet high.

"They finally concluded that domes and spires and parapets were not included in the ordinance," he says, "therefore I could build it forty feet. That solved that problem."

Jerry got the scratch coat of plaster on the walls, then took off for a fishing trip to Canada. "We built it, then we built the plans." He paid a friend five hundred bucks and eventually got a permit that officially allowed the castle as a remodel of an existing agricultural building—an old barn long gone from the property.

Lighting another cigarette and laughing, Jerry says, "Basically I snookered them."

Since then, Jerry's castle has become a landmark.

"Airline pilots I talk to, for Alaska Airlines," Jerry says, "they make a turn when they come in from Seattle. They follow a route that takes them right over the top of the castle. They're announcing it to the passengers and all this shit. I talked to a couple of the pilots, and they said, 'We call that the *Castle Turn into* PDX.' "

The castle's finest hour was in 1993, when a friend's wife sewed huge banners for the place. Four banners hung from the castle keep, and a half-dozen banners hung from the courtyard battlements and parapet towers. The keep's 250-pound door was painted with the castle's crest, a lion, similar to the crest of Norway. All of this, for a very special event.

"My daughter got married here ten years ago. We had a big wedding out here. There was, like, three hundred people." Jerry says, "I had this place dolled up like you wouldn't believe. Big banners and horseshit. Her husband dressed as Robin Hood, and she dressed as Maid Marion. And we had the Society for Creative Anachronism people out here for three days. I set up portable showers, and I had ten porta-potties. Jesus. Dance floors. The whole deal."

Since then the medieval groupies have talked about buying the castle as a permanent headquarters for Renaissance fair events. Another couple tried to buy the castle in order to lease it out for weddings; they'd planned to rent period costumes and provide catering, but Jerry backed away from the deal when it all seemed to be going too fast.

One irony is how a fortress built to exclude strangers now seems to attract a steady stream of the curious.

Jerry lights another Delicato cigarette and says, "We used to have a lot of trouble with people driving in all the time. Christ, one morning I was sitting in the castle having a cup of coffee, and I hear this noise, and the wife comes into the kitchen and says, 'What the hell is going on?' She looked out the little window on the bottom floor, and there's a guy with a forty-foot motor home trying to turn around in the driveway. It took him about half an hour."

He says, "We put up NO TRESPASSING signs, but there must be a lot of illiterate people out there because they don't seem to know what it means."

An independent film company has used the castle as a backdrop for a film about the Middle Ages. Jerry's mother and brother live in the two closest houses. State Farm Insurance has asked about coming out to see just what it is they've insured, but no agent has ever made the trip.

"Rumor has it there's a basement dungeon under the tower," Jerry says, "and I just let people keep thinking that."

He adds, "I'm probably known as a crazy man in Camas, but I don't give a damn what they think."

His castle rises next to a small lake edged with cattails and lawn. This is the flooded quarry where Jerry dug rock for his original construction. That first labor-intensive tower was so solid it took two days to knock it down with a bulldozer. Now the stony ruins of it rise from the depths of the flooded quarry. Near the ruins, the castle's drawbridge spans the lake. The drawbridge used to lift and lower, until Jerry's brother, Ken, came along.

"There's an apparatus up in there with a motor and a series of couplers, and I had cables down," Jerry says. "And I had a guy rig me up a switch. My brother's the one who broke it. He came down here with a couple of his cronies—I was gone—and they were all drunk and messing with the goddamn bridge. They messed the switch up. They were always down here running it. Everybody who came here had to work the goddamn drawbridge."

With Jerry spending every winter fishing in Mexico, the castle is a little worse for wear. Inside the keep, sections of Sheetrock and insulation are pulled down to show dark stains and water damage inside the walls. You can smell mildew in stale air.

"I used a system of downspouts *inside* the walls, which was fine—made out of ABS," he says. "When I did the gutters on top of the building, I used a trough-type system. Then I had to get a downspout through this galvanized metal into my ABS. We had some made, and they worked fine. We used a fiberglass buildup roof and it held up really good, but then we started getting water leaks. This was maybe four years ago. Lo and behold, the galvanized drop out of the gutter had rusted away."

The stucco isn't as white as it used to be. In some places it's cracked and chipping away. In a few spots, the metal lath underneath shows through.

"The worst part is the exterior stucco," Jerry says. "I've coated it twice: the first time, and then I redid it about twelve

71

years ago. I should go around and clean it up. I use water and bleach and spray it. Then it's a matter of batching. You get a mixer and a sprayer and all your material, and you keep mixing and spraying, and it goes pretty fast.

"This place is in pretty rough shape, compared to how it was," he adds. "But it's fixable."

So this is the year for fixing the castle. Among other projects. In the garage is a stripped-down thirty-year-old, twenty-one-foot StarCraft fishing boat. Jerry is installing a metal dragon that will rear up from the bow with a red eye on one side and a green eye on the other. The dragon is plumbed to spit fire. He's adding twelve inches to raise the bow and help the flat-bow boat handle better in rough water.

"I'll have it down in Mexico, and we get into some stuff in the afternoons," he says. "The wind picks up, and you're riding in ten-, twelve-foot waves. It causes you some concern with an open bow."

In retrospect, he says, "My advice would be: Don't do it. It's obvious, looking at the exterior, that stucco is not conducive to this area. They've come out with new exterior stucco material I'm going to use, and it's a hell of a lot better. But I've lived here with women, and they don't like this, and they don't like that, and they don't like going up and down the stairs. That's probably why there's no women here now." And again, he laughs.

Jerry Bjorklund laughs a lot. Far overhead, you can hear the dull roar of a jetliner making the "castle turn" into Portland International Airport.

And it all goes back to that one night, drinking Black Velvet . . .

"The problem is I told somebody I was going to do it," Jerry says. "That was probably my biggest downfall. If I say I'm going to do something, I don't give a damn what it takes."

But that's not to say Jerry Bjorklund has regrets.

"Too many people, to my mind, they do things like everybody else does, and I'm not going to be like that. Never have been." And, again, he lights another Mexican cigarette and laughs his gravelly laugh.

For Roger DeClements—who has built three castles—the first was more about speed and saving money. Born in Edmonds, Washington, Roger worked as a building contractor during the 1970s. Roger has a wife and three children, and because his wife is afraid of doctors, all the kids were born in his castles. The first two kids, in a castle he built in Machias, Washington, five miles north of Snohomish, which is east of Everett, which is north of Seattle. It's a little town named after a town in Maine, with a little white steepled church built in 1902, and it sits in a valley on the Pilchuk River.

"My first castle," Roger says, "I got financing. It was 1980, when interest rates were eighteen percent, and we went to the local banks and nobody was giving loans then. Somebody mentioned Citicorp, so we went to Citicorp, and they said, 'Sure . . . at eighteen percent . . .' "

Still, Citicorp didn't know what their money was financing.

"They didn't even know it was going to be a castle," Roger says. "They just wanted security, so we used another piece of property as collateral. The second castle, we used our own money. This third castle, we used our own money, then when we got farther along we just had a banker come up and look and see it to refinance it.

"The first castle was actually a concrete tilt-up castle. We carved the shape of the walls in the sand, put the rebar in there, poured the concrete in, tilted them up and picked the shape out of the sand. It was a very inexpensive castle and completed in five weeks. I did everything from start to finish."

Basing them on Disneyland castles and castles in movies, Roger drew his own plans.

"In Washington State," he says, "you have to take your plans to a structural engineer and they'll put their stamp on. And then, no problem after that.

"My degree is in chemistry and physics, but I've been doing a lot of architecture and engineering, myself," Roger explains. "And I specialize in castles.

"The first one was a single tower," he says. "Eight hundred square feet on two floors. It was built basically like a basement, with concrete walls we tilted up. Then we insulated by furring out with two-by-fours and doing Sheetrock on the inside. A lot of people across the country, that's how they'll start out building their castles, but I found that doesn't work very well. Plus, everybody was coming out and asking, 'Is that real stone?' So I got so tired of that question."

He adds, "We built it in one day, so it was quite the surprise for the neighborhood. Boom—and there it was.

"Kids would love to sneak down the driveway to see how far they could get before getting too scared. People would love to stop on the road and take pictures."

That first castle cost only $14,000 and took only five weeks from start to finish. It still sits on five acres near the bank of the Pilchuk River. It has electric heat, but what Roger gained in speed and cost, the DeClements family paid for in comfort.

"Furring the walls out with insulation," Roger says, "that doesn't work well. The cold goes right through the concrete. It gets right to where the insulation is. Then the warm inside air filters through the insulation and contacts the cold surface of the concrete or blocks. Then the water will condense. As soon as one water molecule condenses, another one is there to take its place. So you get this continuous condensation on the cold wall behind the insulation. That's a problem, because it will cause mold to grow, and it smells like a basement."

In order to go back to college and study for a graduate degree, Roger sold that castle to artists to use as a studio. "Before I built my second castle, I went back to college and learned a lot," he says. "I was a contractor from '75 until about '87, building homes and commercial buildings, using the traditional methods. Going to college, I learned a lot more about the physical process of what's going on with heat transfer and moisture."

He says, "So for the second castle we built, we went to real stone."

That second castle stands on a rock above a waterfall in Sedro-Woolley, Washington. It's perched on a stone precipice, high above a nature pool where local kids swim all summer. Instead of electric heat, the second castle was heated with a wood stove.

He says, "The second one we designed to look like a castle, and you couldn't tell when it was built. We used all stone and incorporated a new construction method, too, starting with a double-wall castle where you go from rock on the outside, then a layer of rigid, extruded polystyrene, then reinforced concrete, and then you'd go back to stone again, so you couldn't see the concrete or insulation on the inside. All you could see is the stone."

Step-by-step, Roger explains: "The first thing to go up is the rebar grid, then the insulation boards. Then we run the conduit and plumbing, high-speed Internet, whatever you want. Then you build a double rock wall, on the inside and the outside. After you get up about eight feet, you fill it with concrete. Then you do it over again. The two rock walls, which are held together by stainless-steel rods, form a permanent concrete form. It's just like the Romans did a long time ago. They did the same thing. They didn't use metal ties, they used extra-long rocks to tie the two rock walls together.

"We try to find a quarry, where the stones come out rectangular-shaped, ashlar stones, so we're not trying to stack a whole bunch of round stones. It can be done with river rock, but it will take a lot more time, and it won't be quite as strong."

Instead of five acres, the second castle sits on twenty. Instead of five weeks, this castle took Roger from 1992 to 1995 to build.

"The second castle couldn't be seen from the road like the first one could," he says. "It was a little more remote. I got a good deal on the land because the only way to get there was you had to cross this hundred-foot-deep gorge. So I built a metal bridge, then all the materials were hauled over in a wheelbarrow. Sometimes I go back there and I can't believe what I'd done."

Still, Roger DeClements says he loves the work. "A lot of people will come up and say, 'Oh, I can't believe this. I could never do this.' To me, it's basically clear and simple. It's very relaxing to do it. It's very peaceful and relaxing to be out there in the fresh air with the trees and the hills . . . stacking stones."

It's interesting to note here, Carl Jung began to explore his subconscious by playing a building game with stones. Like a puzzle. Putting them together, he felt he was plunged into outer space, where he had visions that would shape the rest of his life.

"It's like doing a jigsaw puzzle," Roger DeClements says. "Getting all the pieces together. But it doesn't strain you or keep your mind going a mile a minute. And then you can get creative, because you can make curves and towers and different shapes with it."

And living in a castle?

"It feels different to live in a castle instead of a house," he says. "It's quiet. It doesn't shake in the wind. The temperature doesn't go up and down with the outside temperature. The stone holds it constant." He adds, "I haven't been able to make the transition to a medieval knight or something. I'm still the same person."

That castle was forty-five feet tall, with arched windows and four thousand square feet of living space on three floors. Still, when it came time to sell and move on, the first two realtors balked. They said there were no comparable sales in the area. Subsequent realtors said not to worry, and they immediately had three full-price offers and sold that castle in 1995 for $425,000.

The search was on for new "castle land." They looked in Utah, but land was too expensive or no water was available. "We went from Logan, we went up to Jackson, to Targee, Sun Valley, and up into Montana to Big Sky, then to over here, and this just beat them all by a mile."

Now, here they are in Bonner County, Idaho, high in the Schweitzer Mountain ski resort.

"You can do plans ahead of time or you can just build," Roger says. "It depends on where you build. Different locations, different cities, different counties have different permit requirements. Some of them can take a couple years to give a permit. Some of them can take ten minutes. That's one reason we like Idaho. They're permit-friendly."

He says, "If you're searching for castle land, I tell a lot of people to go to the county planning department first and ask them. A lot of people will think: 'I want an eighty-foot-tall

77

tower . . .' So they need to check if the county has a thirty-five-foot height restriction, or any architectural requirements."

The Idaho castle, Roger named Castle Kataryna for his daughter, who was born here. It has a winding staircase inside, walnut woodwork, and pointed Gothic doors and windows, many of them stained-glass.

Touring the castle, Roger points out the walnut window frames he made. "In the second castle," he says, "the windows were put in after the walls were built. In this third castle, the windows actually went in right after the rebar and insulation, before the rock goes up around them. That gave us a lot more authentic look and finish. In the second castle, we had to try to cut the boards to fit, then caulk around them. In the third castle, the windows went in first, wrapped in plastic to protect them, stone was built around them, we attached the window frames only to the outside rock layer, which can move and expand. The inside stone layer stays seventy-two degrees, and the outside can go from zero to a hundred, so it gets bigger and smaller. This way the windows will move with the outside. We attach them to the outside because that's where we want to seal them from the weather."

Another improvement with this latest castle is the "hydronic" heating system, where a boiler heats water that runs through piping under the floors. It's even, quiet heat, and the castle's thermal mass of stone will stay warm for three days after the heat is turned off.

In a little room near the castle gates, Roger shows the boiler, saying, "I like it because I couldn't have baseboards or forced-air registers in the *look* of a castle. This hides it, so it's invisible, plus you don't have the noise of the fans coming on."

Between the insulated stone walls and the hydronic heat,

Roger DeClements has evolved his perfect formula for a livable castle. Well, almost perfect . . .

"In the first castle," he says, "I didn't anticipate the problem with the mold. Which is actually a big thing now. A few years ago it was radon, now it's mold in homes. They make homes so tight that they've locked all this moisture in there, and as soon as moisture gets to a cold surface it condenses. With our new method, with the insulation layer inside the wall, the moisture never has the chance to get near it. So my wife complains this castle is too dry. We have twenty feet of snow piled outside, and she says, 'This is too dry.' "

To solve the dry air, he's built a heated swimming pool in the stairwell. There, a waterfall will cascade from the top of a stone newel post. Candles will sit on stone ledges, and the pump and filters will be tucked away in an underwater grotto cave.

Like Jerry Bjorklund, Roger found his wife had some castle ideas of her own. Breaking ground in June of 1999, he'd planned to build the third castle by using a construction boom—much like the tripod of trailer tongues Jerry built— but his wife wouldn't let him cut the trees he'd have to remove to let the boom swing around. So, as with the second castle, Roger carried each stone up by hand.

Now, thanks to his wife, the castle is surrounded by native tamarack trees, cedars and pines and rocky fields of huckleberry bushes. Deer and elk and bear roam the neighborhood. The view goes all the way to the Rocky Mountains and Montana. It's a view Roger's had plenty of time to enjoy.

"I got all the stone up there one stone at a time," he says. "The second castle was built all by hand, carrying the stone over that bridge by wheelbarrow. As we built those double rock walls, we put logs sticking out through the walls on both sides. Then we'd put planks across those. We'd put logs through the walls, then pull them out as we worked our way up. That's actually how they did the old castles. They had a name for them—they called them 'put logs.' If you look at old photos of the castles in Europe you see all these holes in the walls. Of course, some were to shoot arrows out of, but the little holes were where they put these logs so then you don't have scaffolding going all the way up the walls. I had no idea that's how they did it."

After removing the scaffolding "put logs," Roger filled most of the small holes with square stones. Some he left open as vents.

In order to keep building all winter, he enclosed his construction platform in a plywood shed to protect himself from the high mountain wind and snow and the fact he was working on a sheer wall that rose five stories above a steep hillside.

"When it was five degrees outside," Roger says, "I kept laying stone all winter."

He and a second man lifted the long, eight-by-eight rough-cut Douglas fir beams—one end at a time—into the beam slots. He studded the inside walls with chunks of semiprecious stone. Amethyst. Citrine. Rose quartz. Green calcite. Clear quartz crystals. He hand-carved decorative patterns in the kitchen cabinets and embedded stained-glass mosaics in the masonry walls. On the second floor, he points out a metal statue on the fireplace mantel.

"See the dragon?" Roger says. "A castle has got to have a dragon."

In the bright mountain light, the narrow stained-glass windows blaze bright as red, blue, and yellow neon. In some windows, the colored glass panels are sealed between the layers of clear double-paned windows. Other windows, the stained glass is the only glass in the frame.

"Some windows," Roger says, "I had to go back to the traditional, where I just had to touch the stained glass. The double-paned I try to stay away from as much as I can. When you look at the moon, you can kind of see a double moon. If I can just use solid glass, you can see the moon the way it is."

Battlements are lined with sharp spires of Columbia River basalt. The ceilings are twelve feet high. All the windows are built into pointed Gothic archways in the stone walls.

"You follow the windows with the stones until you get to the point the stones are going to fall down," Roger explains. "Higher than that, the stones are just propped up by sticks. A bigger window, when I get to the top I actually make a small form to do the peak on. A few sticks will hold some rocks, but it's much faster to use a form. You can stack the stones up, and just pull the form out."

He adds, "If you bump one of the sticks, then . . . the rocks will start coming down."

From the windows to the stonework to the built-in vacuum cleaner system to the wood shingles on the conical tower roofs, Roger DeClements did it all. He wrote his name and the date on the trusses inside the roof. And he followed the ancient mason's tradition of sealing his chisel and trowel inside the walls when he was done laying stone. But by accident. The tools actually fell between the two layers of stone and he buried them with the concrete he poured to fill the space in the permanent form.

Still, despite all this work, Castle Kataryna isn't quite done. There's still the drawbridge to build. Another twenty pallets—thirty-two tons—of stone will soon be delivered by a Canadian quarry. With enough money, Roger plans to build a "great hall" farther uphill, behind the current castle, then connect the two buildings with battlement walls that will enclose a courtyard similar to Jerry Bjorklund's castle plan.

Beyond that, Roger DeClements is already looking for new land for a fourth castle. He wants to learn ironworking, and build a medieval village around his next project.

"The first three were mostly just castle keeps," he says, "where the king and queen would live. I haven't been able to build the big courtyard walls and the big entrance towers and gates to make a castle twenty thousand square feet. The next time, I want to have a big great hall with timbers like a cathedral. And courtyard walls going around. I've got the plans in my head and a little bit down on paper."

He adds, "We looked on the Oregon coast and it was out of our budget."

And Roger DeClements isn't the only person looking to build his dream castle. Since posting a website for Castle Kataryna on the Internet, he's become the nation's guru for private castle projects. People from every state have contacted him for advice about how to build their own fantasy projects.

"With the Web," he says, "I'm getting all these people contacting me. I never realized there were so many people with the passion for castles. They love them. Lots of people say, 'It's been my dream for years to build a castle.' And it's not just men, it's the women, too, who have this same dream."

As the point man for the new American castle movement, he says, "The attraction is a love of the romantic era of castles people envision. The better life they picture back then. There's a whole group called the SCA [Society for Creative Anachronism] that like to create the medieval times as they thought they should've been. Not as they were, but as they picture these times in their minds, their fantasies. Also, the movies and the Disney castles have inspired people to want castles, too."

As a practical building contractor, he says, "Besides, the lifespan of so many houses is getting smaller and smaller with the new materials being invented."

Now people from Alaska to Florida are learning from his mistakes.

"When I originally put this castle on the Internet, on a website, I was flooded with orders to build castles all over the United States. There are very few people who have the patience and the time to stack all that stone. And have the knowledge to do it right.

"There are a lot of people who are building castles for themselves, the way I first did. You build a block or concrete shell and then fur it out and insulate it, but I don't recommend that at all. It's just a basement that ends up smelling damp."

In response, Roger does what he can. "People often call me to ask questions and tell me about their projects," he says, "and I try to coach them, but most of them will go back to the old way because they have to cut cost. It just really hurts them in the long run, because then they find out the hard way."

He adds, "So I end up doing a lot of consulting on castle problems."

Despite the castle's million-dollar price, the DeClements family isn't rich. Roger works as a real estate agent with Windemere Realty, at the nearby ski resort, and during most of this last castle's construction the family of six—his kids are three, six and ten years old, plus his wife and a child from her previous marriage—have lived on just the second floor, sharing about a thousand square feet of living space.

Roger says, "My kids are kind of getting tired of all the

other kids poking fun at them, wanting to come up and see their castle. They kind of want to be in a normal house so it doesn't attract so much attention." He adds, "My wife, she gets a little bugged with people always coming up. Because it attracts people. But I love talking to them. What strikes me is how many of them say, 'We've just been to Europe looking at castles . . .' I don't know if that's just coincidence or if I'm just attracting more of that type."

It seems odd, but for three men with such similar passions, living relatively close together, Jerry Bjorklund and Roger DeClements and Bob Nippolt have never met. They've never seen each other's castles. It's only a few hours' drive from castle to castle, but they've never even heard about each other.

Working in a mental hospital, Carl Jung noticed that all insane people drew their delusions from a limited stock of images and ideas. These he called "archetypes" and argued these images are inherited and held in common by all people over all time. Through Jung's writing and painting, and later his own castle building—his "confession in stone"—Jung was able to examine and record his subconscious life.

None of these three castle builders has ever heard of Carl Jung.

Near the Columbia Gorge, the border between Washington State and Oregon, about seven miles up from the mouth of the White Salmon River, another castle looms among the mountains. Unlike the DeClements castle, this one rises from a rocky point in a valley floor, at a bend in the rushing, white-water river. It's sixty-five feet tall, four floors rising from a basement dug into the bedrock. A vertical maze of stairs and balconies with a secret room.

Retired from the military and a second career as a commercial jetliner pilot, Bob Nippolt has a full head of thick white hair. He's a slight figure wearing jeans and tennis shoes and black-framed glasses. These days, after years of climbing the castle stairs, he walks a little stiff-legged. His ancestors were Irish, and he practices the bagpipes. Summer nights, he sleeps outdoors on the castle terrace above the river.

In the living room of his castle, a framed black-and-white photo sits on a side table. It shows a building made of rough stone.

"My great grandfather came from around Cork in Ireland," Bob says, holding the photograph, "and he built this house out of stone in North Dakota. He must've come out to North Dakota in the 1870s. It is since in ruins, but the historical society is trying to restore it."

About his own building project, Bob says, "I don't know why I wanted to build a castle. I just saw some pictures of some gatehouses. And I'd seen some gatehouses in Ireland and Scotland, and I thought it would be kind of fun. Then I got carried away. I went crazy."

Beginning in 1988, he built his 4,800-square-foot castle out of rough-faced concrete block. Rising four floors with a basement, the walls are twenty inches thick, consisting of two rows of eight-inch-thick block with a space of about four inches between them. For reinforcement, a grid of three-quarter-inch steel rebar holds each wall, and every third row of blocks is filled solid with concrete. For insulation, the hollow inside the walls is filled with vermiculite. That four-inch hollow also holds the wiring conduit and plumbing.

Like Roger DeClements's castle, the heat comes from water heated in a basement boiler and routed through pipes in the concrete floor.

Steel beams support the first floor. Upper floors rest on closely spaced eight-by-twelve beams.

Bob will tell you, "I bought all the beams at a sale in Salem, Oregon, when a company had gone broke. I went down and looked at them and bought the whole two truckloads. I thought . . . *I'll use them for something.* At that time, it occurred to me to build the castle."

He adds, "I should never have found those beams."

First he built a teepee across the small lake from his future castle site. He lived in his wood shake teepee the entire time he was building.

Much of what Bob built with came here—like Bob himself—from a previous life somewhere else. "I read the want ads all the time," he says. "A lot of this stuff here is old planks and old lumber that we ran through the planer right here."

The beams came from a bankruptcy sale. The steel roof came from an old Standard Oil building being torn down. The bathroom vanities are antique dressers with a hole cut in the top for a recessed sink. The bar is from the old East Ave Tavern in Portland, Oregon. All the insulation he got for free from a Safeway supermarket being remodeled.

Like Roger's castle, the windows and doors are pointed Gothic arches—including a tall stained-glass mural inside the spiral stairwell. There are no curtains, but there are no neighbors, either. The floors are stone: slate from China or nearby Mount Adams.

Laying the concrete-block walls, he worked with an old mason who did near-perfect work. "He was slow," Bob remembers, "but he knew the business. When we got to the top floor, our roof was only off by three-eighths of an inch. This place was absolutely square."

Unlike Jerry Bjorklund, height wasn't an issue with local planners in Klickitat County. "They really didn't bother me about height," Bob says. "*Now* they would. *Now* they're pretty particular. And because I have so many code violations inside the house—like the stairwell, where I don't meet specifications—for my final inspection, they came out here and said, 'Bob, we'd just as soon you never got a final inspection.' That's where we left that."

Even without the final official sign-off, he's confident he's inside the law. "My original permit goes back so far," Bob says. "Since then the rules have changed, so I'm grandfathered under an older disposition as far as the county inspections are concerned."

But going up to sixty-five feet did complicate some details. "The wiring," he says, "is all inside conduit. It had to be. By the time I got to the place I was going to put my electricity in, the inspector said it was a commercial building because it was over three floors, so everything has to be in conduit. Otherwise, I probably wouldn't use it, but now I'm glad I did." Like the DeClements castle, tall evergreen trees stand so near the castle walls the gutters have to be cleaned of their needles. It's a terrifying job, so high up, but with forest fires a threat, it has to be done. Still, with the river so close and a constant, heavy flow of water from the natural artesian well, Bob's not too worried.

"The fire danger is modest to light because of the situation along the river," he says. "Nobody camps here because the government owns most of the surrounding land. But fire is one of the reasons why I went with concrete and steel."

All day long, in good weather, people raft and kayak past the west side of the castle. The river's rushing babble is the background sound to every minute here.

"See that rock over there?" Bob says, pointing at the steep cliffs on the opposite side of the White Salmon River. "It's the same kind of rock over here. So when I put my foundation in, I was right on bedrock. When the guy came to inspect my foundation, he said, 'What the hell are you expecting? Are you going to make a bomb shelter?' I said, 'If the river ever comes up, it's not going to take my house out.'"

And Bob Nippolt's glad he did. "In 1995, they had a hundred-year flood," he says. "The river crested four or five feet from right here. There were logs and chairs and everything in the world coming downstream."

With its bomb-shelter basement and huge beams, Bob admits most of his house is overbuilt. Getting it done took seven or eight years of less-than-continuous work. "I'd shut down in the wintertime," Bob says, "or I'd run out of money."

Unlike Jerry, Bob found bankers were willing to lend him money for his dream.

"I don't think financing was a problem," he says. "I have a loan through Countrywide—they were very happy to finance me. Earlier on, I had a local bank finance me. At that time, the house was fairly well known. As far as fire and things, it's pretty impervious to most disasters."

Those "disasters" include the parties. "I feel my house is just about impervious to people, too," Bob says. "I've been here with three hundred people all dancing in the living room."

Then there are always the uninvited guests. Pointing out water stain on the white inside walls, Bob says, "A rodent got in the bottom of the downspout, and the pipe filled up and broke off and the water was directed into my unfinished top floor So I did get water throughout the house."

Instead of concrete block, the inside walls are finished with rough plaster painted white. "To make it look like wattle," Bob says, "first we put plaster on with the straw mixed in, but that wasn't working. Then we found out that if we cut the straw into about six-to-eight-inch lengths, then put the plaster on, then patted the straw into the wet plaster, then we got fairly close to what we wanted."

Pointing out the three chimneys—two for fireplaces, and one for the basement oil-fired boiler—he says, "Last winter I came home from Hood River and there was a large animal behind the TV, moving. That's the day a duck had flown down the flue. He came down to the fireplace and into the house. I had a hell of a time getting him out."

And like Jerry and Roger, he gets the curious people. Bob says, "A few times in the summertime people show up. It's mostly because I have so many friends in the area. They all say, 'Oh well, Bob doesn't care. Let's go see Bob.'"

He adds, "And it works—long as they bring whiskey."

In an odd coincidence, MTV contacted both Bob Nippolt and Roger DeClements about renting their castles to film an episode of the television show *Reel World*. Roger told them no. Bob liked the idea, but it was too late in the season for the network to get motel rooms in the area for its fifty-person production team.

At this time, the top floor is unfinished. Wide arched windows look out over the stone terraces far below. "I'm not afraid of heights," Bob says. "I've parachuted and hang-glided. Heights don't bother me. The only thing that bothers me now is I don't have any knees left. I'm not as agile as I was."

This year, he's planting his twenty-six acres with hay and trees in order to qualify for lower property taxes. He's building a massive new front entry that supports a stone patio off the second-floor bedrooms.

What he'd like to do is build a second wing, a glassed-in dining room off the kitchen. And he'd like to replace the windows he made by hand in the basement, taking apart and re-using the parts of Andersen windows he got cheap. For the outside windowsills, he wishes he'd used concrete sill block instead of construction-grade foam.

"Because I was just making the place for myself. I probably should've designed for a lot more closet space," he says in retrospect. "And rather than a square stairway, I should've done a circular stairway. I should've taken the time to make a masonry stairway. There's one book. It's a large book, it's called *The History of the British House*, and it goes into windows, doors, ironwork, how the doors were made . . . I didn't have that book before I started. Had I had that book, I would've done a lot of things differently. And I would've taken more time."

And a little more money . . . "The truth of the matter is," he says, "a lot of the stuff I put in the house, since it was just for myself, I didn't go to first-line stuff."

He wishes he'd dug a moat around the castle.

He wants to put a new surface of crushed oyster shell on the bocci ball court.

And the naked mannequin that overlooks the river from a bedroom balcony, well, her fiberglass skin is cracked and faded. "I was going to take her to Portland," Bob says, "and get a boob job for her."

Soon enough, all those details won't matter. Because this year Bob's selling the place. For the next owner, the good news is that eight or nine local contractors know Bob's place inside and out. "The bathrooms are all stacked," he says. "And there are guys around here, who live in Hood River, who worked on this house, did the plumbing and electricity and know it all. They're avid windsurfers, so they're not going anywhere."

Neither are the countless birds or the river. Or his castle. Or the stories, the local legends about it.

Whether castle building is a bid for immortality or a

hobby—a "fun" way to kill time—whether it's a gift to the future or a memorial to the past, in the hills above Camas, Washington, Jerry Bjorklund's castle is still the landmark where jetliners know to turn. In the mountains of Idaho, skiers still discover Roger DeClements's Castle Kataryna, a monument to his daughter. A vision in the snow. Just like the castle so many people have always dreamed of building.

Their own confession in stone. Their memoir.

In the valley of the White Salmon River, the water still rushes past the tall gray tower. The wind and the birds still move between the trees. Even if a forest fire sweeps through, for the next hundred years this pile of stone will still stand here.

Only Bob Nippolt is leaving.

For now, all three castles remain unfinished.

{Frontiers}

"If everybody jumped off a cliff," my father used to say, "would *you?*"

This was a few years ago. It was the summer a wild cougar killed a jogger in Sacramento. The summer my doctor wouldn't give me anabolic steroids.

A local supermarket used to offer this special deal: if you brought in fifty bucks' worth of receipts, you could buy a dozen eggs for a dime, so my best friends, Ed and Bill, used to stand in the parking lot asking people for their receipts. Ed and Bill, they ate blocks of frozen egg white, ten-pound blocks they got at a bakery supply house, egg albumen being the most easily assimilated protein.

Ed and Bill used to make these road trips to San Diego, then cross the border on foot at Tijuana with the rest of the gringo day-trippers to buy their steroids, their Dianabol, and smuggle it back.

This must've been the summer the DEA had other priorities.

Ed and Bill are not their real names.

We were road-tripping down through California, and we stopped in Sacramento to visit some friends, except nobody was home. We waited a whole afternoon beside their pool. Ed's bleached crew cut was growing out, so he leaned over the edge of their deck and asked me to just shave his head.

At this point the cougar was still running wild. This was the countryside, but not. The wilderness platted into 2.5-acre mini-estates. Somewhere was a female cougar with cubs, squeezed in among the soccer moms and swimming pools.

This was less of a vacation than a pilgrimage from one Gold's Gym franchise to the next along the West Coast. On the road, we bought water-packed tuna and ate it dry, tossing the empty cans in the backseat. We washed it down with diet soda and farted the length of Interstate 5.

Ed and Bill shot preloaded syringes of D-ball, and I did everything else. Arginine, ornithine, smilax, Inosine, DHEA, saw palmetto, selenium, chromium, free-range New Zealand sheep testicle, Vanadyl, orchid extract . . .

At the gym, while my friends bench-pressed three times their body weight, pumping up, shredding their clothes from the inside, I'd hover around their giant elbows.

"You know," I'd say, "I think I'm putting on some real size with this yohimbe bark tincture."

Yeah, *that* summer.

The only reason they let me hover was for contrast.

It's the old strategy of choosing ugly bridesmaids so the bride looks better.

Mirrors are only the methadone of bodybuilding. You need a real audience. There's that joke: How many bodybuilders does it take to screw in a lightbulb?

Three—one to screw in the bulb and two to say, "Really, dude, you look massive!"

Yeah, *that* joke. It's not really a joke.

The Sacramento people we tried to visit, on our way home from Mexico we stopped by their house again. They were throwing a barbecue for some friends who'd been away at a men's retreat.

On this retreat, somebody explained, each man was sent out into the desert to wander until he had a revelation. Now while the tiki torches flickered and the propane barbecue smoked, one man stood clutching some kind of shriveled baseball bat. It was the desiccated skeleton of a dead cactus he'd found on his vision quest, but it was more.

"I realized," he said, "that this cactus skeleton was me. This was my manhood, abrasive and hard on the outside, but brittle and hollow."

He'd brought the skeleton home on the airplane, in his lap.

Everybody else around the deck closed their eyes and nodded. Except my friends, who turned the other way with their jaws clenched to keep from laughing. Their huge arms folded across their chests, they elbowed each other and wanted to walk up the road to see some historical rock.

The hostess stopped us at the gate and said, "Don't! Just don't."

Clutching her wine cooler and looking into the darkness

beyond the steam of the whirlpool and the light of the tiki torches, not looking at us, she said a cougar had been prowling around. The cougar had been right up next to their deck, and she showed us in the shrubs a scattering of short, coarse, blond hair.

That year, everywhere we drove, that whole trip, there were already fences and property lines and names on everything.

Ed juiced and lifted for a couple more years until he blew out his knees. Bill, until he ruptured a disk in his back.

It wasn't until last year, when my father died, that my doctor finally came across. I lost weight and kept losing weight until he whipped out his prescription pad and said, "Let's try you on thirty days of Anadrol."

So I jumped off the cliff, too.

People squinted at me and asked what was different. My arms got a little bigger around, but not that much. More than the size, the feeling was enough. I stood straight, my shoulders squared.

According to the package insert, Anadrol (oxymetholone) is an anabolic steroid, a synthetic derivative of testosterone. Possible side effects include: testicular atrophy, impotence, chronic priapism, increased or decreased libido, insomnia, and hair loss. One hundred tablets cost eleven hundred bucks. Insurance does not cover it.

But the feeling. Your eyes are popped open and alert. The way women look so good when they're pregnant, glowing and soft and so much more female—Anadrol makes you look and feel that much more male. The raging priapism part, that was the first couple weeks. You are nothing but the real estate between your legs. It's the same as those old illustrations in *Alice in Wonderland*, where she's eaten the cake marked "Eat Me" and grown until her arm sticks out the front door. Except it's not your arm that sticks out, and wearing Spandex bicycle pants is totally out of the question.

About the third week, the priapism subsided, or seemed to spread to my entire body. Weight lifting gets better than sex. A workout becomes an orgy. You're having orgasms—cramping, hot, rushing orgasms in your delts, your quads, your lats and traps. You forget about that lazy old penis. Who needs it. In a way it's a peace, an escape from sex. A vacation from libido. You might see a hot woman and think, "Grrrrrrr," but your next egg white omelette or set of squats is a lot more attractive.

I didn't go into this stupid. This is a kind of weird aside, but a friend in medical school made me a deal that if I introduced her to Brad Pitt, she'd sneak me in to help her dissect some cadavers. She met Brad, and I spent a long night helping her disassemble dead bodies so first-year premed students could study them. Our third cadaver was a sixty-year-old physician. He had the muscle mass and definition of a man in his twenties, but when we opened his chest, his heart was almost the size of his head. I held his chest open and my friend poured in Formalin until his lungs floated. My friend looked at his freaking big heart, and his equally freaky-big dick, and told me: testosterone. Self-administered for years.

She showed me the coiled little wires and the pacemaker buried in his chest and told me he had a history of heart attack after heart attack.

About this same time, a national bodybuilding magazine ran an occasional little feature in its back pages. It wasn't in every issue, and it wasn't in very many, but each feature was a catch-up profile about a star bodybuilder from the 1980s. These were the guys that Ed and Bill wanted to become. Back then, these stars posed and gave interviews swearing they were blessed with great genetics and determination, they just worked hard and ate well, they never used steroids. They swore.

In the update features, these same guys were pale and doughy, battling health problems from diabetes to cancer. And they admitted they had been using steroids, and monkeying with their insulin levels, and shooting human growth hormone.

I knew all this, and I still jumped off the cliff.

My friends didn't stop me. They only told me to eat enough protein to make the investment worthwhile. Still, I didn't buy the ten-pound blocks of egg white. I never filled my fridge with rows and rows of foil-wrapped boneless, skinless chicken breasts and baked potatoes the way Ed and Bill used to. The way they used to stock up for each steroid cycle like it was a six-week siege. I wasn't that dedicated.

I just took the little white pills and worked out and one day in the shower, I noticed my nuts were disappearing.

Okay, I'm sorry. I promised a lot of friends I wouldn't go here, but this was the turning point. When the old goose eggs shrink to Ping-Pong balls, then to marbles, then your doctor asks if you want a refill on your Anadrol script, it's easy to say no.

Here you are, looking great, bright and alert, pumped and ripped, you're looking more like a man than you ever have, but you're less of a man where it counts. You're becoming the simulacrum of masculinity.

Besides, going into this, the appeal of being a freaky, massive pile of muscle had already started to wane. Sure, at first it would be fun, like owning a rambling Victorian mansion covered in gingerbread trim; but after the first couple weeks the constant maintenance would eat up my life. I could never wander very far from a gym. I'd be eating egg protein every hour. All this, and the whole project would still collapse some day.

My father was dead, Ed and Bill were a mess, and I was fast losing faith in tangible shit. Tangible, temporal shit. Here I'd written a story, a make-believe book, and it was making me more money than any real work I'd ever done. I had about a thirty-day window of free time between my book obligations and the opening of the *Fight Club* movie. Here was a thirty-day experiment, an updated Jack London adventure packaged in a little brown bottle.

I jumped off the cliff because it was an adventure.

And for thirty days I felt complete. But just until the tiny white pills ran out. Temporarily permanent. Complete and independent of everything. Everything except the Anadrol.

The woman in Sacramento, hosting that barbecue all those years ago, she'd said, "Those friends of yours, they're crazy."

Beside the swimming pool, the man cradled the brittle cactus skeleton of his masculinity, the woman still stared at her clumps of bleached "cougar fur" that I had trimmed off Ed's crew cut. Pumped and huge in their tank tops, Ed and Bill disappeared, lumbering down the road. Out in the dark was the cougar. Or other cougars.

The hostess said, "Why do men have to do such stupid things?"

"As long as America has a frontier," Thomas Jefferson used to say, "there will be a place for America's misfits and adventurers."

Now Ed and Bill are fat eyesores, but that summer, really, dude, they were massive. A good pump . . . my father . . . the Anadrol . . . all that's left is the intangible story. The legend.

And, okay, that thing about frontiers, maybe it wasn't Thomas Jefferson, but you get the idea.

There will always be cougars outside. It's such a chick thing to think life should just go on forever.

{The People Can}

You go to sea tired. After all the business of scraping and painting the hull, loading provisions, replacing equipment, and stocking parts, after you take an advance on your pay and maybe prepay your rent for the three months you won't be home, after you settle your affairs, you leave "sell" orders with your broker, you say goodbye to your family at the gate of King's Bay Naval Base, you maybe shave your head because it's a long time until you'll see a barber, after all that rushing around, the first few days at sea are quiet.

Inside "the people can" or "locked in the tube" as submariners call their patrol, it's a culture of quiet. In the exercise area, the free weights are coated in thick black rubber. Between the weight plates of the Universal equipment are red rubber pads. Officers and crew wear tennis shoes, and holding almost everything—from plumbing to the running treadmill, anywhere metal meets metal—are rubber isolators to prevent rattling or drumming. The chairs have a thick rubber cap on each leg. Off watch, you listen to music on headphones. The USS *Louisiana,* SSBN-743, is coated to deaden enemy sonar and stay hidden, but any loud, sharp noise they make might be heard by someone listening within twenty-five miles.

"When you go to the bathroom," says the *Louisiana*'s supply officer, Lieutenant Patrick Smith, "you need to lower the seat in case the ship makes a funny roll. A slamming lid could give us away."

"They don't all go at once," says the executive officer, Pete Hanlon, as he describes what happens if the ship changes depth with toilet seats left open. "You'll be on the bridge and hear *WANG!* Then *WANG!* Then *WANG!* One after another, and you'll see the captain getting tighter and tighter."

At any point, a third of the crew may be asleep, so during a patrol the only overhead light in each bunk room is the small red fluorescent light near the curtained doorway. Almost all you hear is the rush of air in the ventilation system. Each crew bunk holds nine berths, triple-deckers, in a U-shape facing the doorway. Each berth, called a "rack," has a six-inch-thick foam mattress that may or may not be dented by your alternate on the submarine's alternate crew. Two crews alternate taking the *Louisiana* on patrol, the Gold Crew and the Blue Crew. If the guy who sleeps in your rack while you're in port weighs 250 pounds and leaves a dent, says Gold Crew mess management specialist Andrew Montroy, then you stuff towels under it. Each berth lifts to reveal a four-inch-deep storage space you call a "coffin locker." Heavy burgundy curtains close each bunk off from the rest. At the head of each mattress is a reading light and a panel with an outlet and controls for a stereo headset similar to the system used on passenger airliners. You have four different types of music from a system that plays compact discs brought on board by the crew. You have volume and balance controls. You have an air vent. Also at the head of each rack is an oxygen mask.

"The biggest fear we have on board is fire," says Lieutenant Smith. "The reason for that is smoke."

In the case of a fire, in narrow passageways full of smoke and without lights, in the pitch darkness, you'd pull the breathing mask and canvas flash hood over your face and you'd feel along the floor for your next breath. On the floor are dark, abrasive patches, square and triangular patches. You'll Braille the floor with your feet until you find a patch. A square patch means an air port you can hook into directly overhead. Triangular patches point to air ports on the wall. You'll plug into the port, take a breath, shout "Air," and then move down the passageway to the next port for your next breath. An outlet coming off the mask lets another crewman hook up to you and breathe as you breathe. You shout "Air" so nobody is alarmed by the loud hiss of air as you disconnect from a port.

To make the *Louisiana* a home, Lieutenant Smith brings whole-bean Gevalia coffee, a coffee grinder, and an espresso machine. Other crewmen bring their own towels, they bring photos to tape on the underside of the bunk above theirs. Montroy brings his thirty favorite CDs. They bring videotapes of life at home. One crewman brings a Scooby-Doo pillowcase. A lot bring their own quilts or blankets.

"I call it my *security blanket*," says Gold Crew storekeeper first class Greg Stone, who writes a diary he can read to his wife later, while she reads hers to him.

You go into the water with only the air that's in the submarine. This same air is cleaned with heated amine, which bonds to the carbon dioxide and removes it. To generate new oxygen, you use 1,050 amps of electricity to split molecules of demineralized seawater. The carbon dioxide and the hydrogen are vented into the surrounding ocean. You use three thousand pounds of hydraulic pressure to compress onboard garbage into sixty-pound, steel-wrapped canisters—about four hundred for each patrol—which you jettison.

You can't drink alcohol, and you can smoke only in the area near the twelve-cylinder Firbank Morris diesel auxiliary engine, called the "Rocker Crusher." The diesel engine acts as backup to the nuclear power plant, the "Pot-Belly Stove."

If you're a crewman, you sleep as little as six feet away from the twenty-four Trident nuclear missiles that fill the center third of the ship, stored in tubes that run from the bilge up through all four decks. Outside the bunk rooms, the missile tubes are painted shades of orange, lighter orange toward the bow and darker toward the stern, to help crewmen with their depth perception in the hundred-foot-long compartment. Mounted on the missile tubes are lockers full of video movies and candy for sale by the Rec Club.

You're surrounded by colored pipes and valves. Purple means refrigerant. Blue, fresh water. Green, seawater. Orange, hydraulic fluid. Brown, carbon dioxide. White, steam. Tan, low-pressure air.

According to Hanlon, Smith, and Gold Crew chief of boat Ken Biller, depth perception is not a problem despite the fact that you'll never focus your eyes farther than the length of the center missile compartment. According to a crewman drinking coffee on the mess deck, your first day back in the sunshine you squint and wear sunglasses, and the Navy recommends you not drive a car for your first two days ashore because of possible problems with depth perception.

Mounted on a couple missile tubes are brass plaques to mark the time and place a missile was fired. On tube number five, a plaque marks the DASO launch on December 18, 1997, at 1500 hours. Blue Crew fired the missile.

"Once in a while," Gold Crew Lieutenant Smith says, "a boat is lucky enough to shoot its missile."

Gold Crew has never fired one.

There are no windows or portholes or cameras mounted outside the hull. Except for the sonar, you are blind in the event you're ever attacked by a . . .

". . . by a giant squid?" Lieutenant Smith says, completing the thought with raised eyebrows. "So far, that hasn't happened."

"We did hit a whale once," says Gold Crew machinist first mate Cedric Daniels. "Well, there are stories about it."

Unexplained bumps against the hull have been explained as whales. On the sonar, deep under water, you can listen to the calls of whales and dolphins and porpoises. The clicking racket made by schools of shrimp. These are noises the crew calls "biologicals."

You go to sea with 720 pounds of coffee, 150 gallons of boxed milk, 900 dozen large eggs, 6,000 pounds of flour, 1,200 pounds of sugar, 700 pounds of butter, 3,500 pounds of potatoes. This is all packed in "food modules," lockers measuring five by five by six and a half feet tall, filled in warehouses ashore and lowered into the ship through a hatch. You go with 600 movie videos, 13 torpedoes, 150 crewmen, 15 officers, and 165 "halfway boxes."

Before departure, the family of each man on board gives

Chief of Boat Ken Biller a shoe-box-sized package, and on the night that marks the halfway point in the patrol, called Halfway Night, Biller distributes the boxes. Smith's wife sends photos and beef jerky and a toy motorcycle to remind him of his own bike onshore. Greg Stone gets a pillowcase printed with a photograph of his wife, Kelley. Biller's wife sends pictures of his dog and his gun collection.

Also on Halfway Night, you can bid for an officer as they're auctioned off. The money goes to the Rec Fund, and the auctioned officers work the next watch for the winning bidders.

Another Halfway Night tradition is auctioning pies. Each winning bidder gets to call the man of his choice to a chair in front of the whole crew and smacks the guy with the pie.

Everybody on board calls Supply Officer Smith "Chop" because the gold insignia on his collar, which are supposed to look like oak leaves, look more like pork chops. Chief of Boat Keller is called "Cob." Chief Executive Officer Hanlon is called "XO." A member of the original crew, like Mess Management Specialist Lonnie Becker, is a "plank owner." You don't watch a movie, you "burn a flick." A door is a hatch. A hat, a "cover." A missile, a "boomer." In the new and politically corrected Navy, the dark-blue coveralls crewmen wear while on patrol are no longer called "poopie suits." Crewmen who serve on the mess deck are no longer "mess cranks." Sauerbraten is not "donkey dick." Ravioli isn't "pillows of death." Creamed chipped beef on toast isn't "shit on a shingle." Corned beef is not "baboon ass."

Not officially. But still you hear it.

Hamburgers and cheeseburgers are still "sliders." Patties of chicken meat are still "chicken wheels." Bunks are "racks" because of the racks that held hammocks on sailing ships. A bathroom is still a "head," named after the holes in the bow of those ships. Two holes for the crew, one for the officers, cut in the heaving, wave-washed deck above the keel.

As XO Hanlon says. "Those guys, they didn't need toilet paper."

Another landmark night during patrol is "Jefe Café." Pronounced hef-AY, and Spanish for "Boss's Café," on this night the officers cook for the crew. They turn off the lights on the mess deck and wait on the crewmen with chemical glow sticks on the tables instead of candles. There's even a maître d'.

For religion, there are "lay leaders," crewmen who can lead Protestant or Catholic services. At Christmas, sailors string lights in their bunk rooms and put up small folding foil trees. They decorate the officers' dining room, the Ward Room, with snowflakes and garlands.

When you go to sea aboard the USS *Louisiana*, this is your life. Crewmen live on an eighteen-hour cycle. Six hours per watch. Six hours' sleep. And six hours off watch, when you can relax, exercise, and study PC-based correspondence courses toward an associate's degree. Every week or so, you sleep an eight-hour "equalizer." The average age of crewmen is twenty-eight. From your bunkroom, you go to the head in your shorts or a towel. Otherwise, most sailors wear their coveralls.

Officers live on a twenty-four-hour cycle. You do not salute officers while on patrol.

"After we're locked in the tube," says Lieutenant Smith, "this is our family, and that's the way we treat them."

Smith points out the framed Pledge of Service on the mess deck wall and says, "A guy can have a great day, but if he comes through here to eat and the service is lousy, the food is lousy, the plates aren't hot, if we don't provide him with that at-home atmosphere, we can ruin his whole day."

Your last few days on patrol, everybody gets "channel fever." You don't want to sleep. You just want to get home. At this point, there are always movies going, with pizza and snacks out around the clock.

On shore, the wives and significant others are raffling off the "first kiss." All the money from the pies and auctions and raffles goes toward the crew party to celebrate coming home.

And the day the USS *Louisiana* arrives home, the families will be on the pier with signs and banners. The commanding officer is always the first ashore, to greet the commodore, but after that . . .

The winner of the raffle is announced and that man and that woman, in front of everyone, they kiss. And everyone else cheers.

POSTSCRIPT: The photographer for this piece, Amy Eckert, jumped through a lot of government hoops to make it happen for *Nest* magazine. She warned me that, since *Nest* was a "design" magazine, the Navy brass seemed worried it had a homosexual reading audience and the piece would be a big exposé about homo activity in a submarine setting.

The photographer stressed how I was never to broach the subject of anal submarine sex. Funny, but until she mentioned it, I'd never even thought about the issue. I was more interested in the slang vocabulary specific to submariners. I wanted to build a picture of very unique words. Slang is the writer's palette of colors. It broke my heart when, before the article was published, Navy censors removed all the slang, including "donkey dick" and "baboon ass."

Still, the sex phobia became the big invisible elephant that was hard to ignore.

One day, in a tight passageway, I was standing with a junior officer as sailors squeezed past, doing their job. My hands were down at my waist, trying to take notes as we talked.

Apropos of nothing, the officer says, "By the way, Chuck, when guys rub up against you like that, it doesn't mean anything."

Until then I hadn't even noticed. Now it meant something. All that rubbing.

Another day, on the mess deck after lunch sailors were sitting around, talking about the problems of allowing women to serve aboard submarines. One man said it would only be a matter of time before two people fell in love, somebody ended up pregnant, and they'd have to scrub a ninety-day mission to return to port.

To this I said no way. I'd been on board long enough to see how cramped their life was. No way, I said, could two people find the room and the privacy to have sex on board.

And another sailor crossed his arms over his chest, leaned back in his chair, and said, "Oh, it happens!" Loud and clear, he smirked and said, "It happens *a lot!*"

Then he realized what he'd said. He'd acknowledged the invisible elephant.

Every man in the room was glaring at him.

What followed was the longest moment of angry silence in Navy history.

Another time, I was asked to wait in a hallway, across from a bulletin board with the day's announcements. The first item was a list of new crewmen and a note to welcome them aboard.

The second item was a heads-up that Mother's Day was coming.

The third item said that "personnel self-harm" was at an all-time high aboard submarines. It said: "Preventing self-harm of personnel aboard submarines is the Navy's highest priority." Creepy Navy-talk for suicide. Another invisible elephant.

The day I left the Kings Bay Naval Base, an officer asked me to write a good piece. I stood, looking at the sub for the last time, and he said fewer and fewer people saw the value in the type of service he valued most.

I saw the value. I admire those people and the job they do.

But by hiding the hardships they endure, it seems the Navy cheats these men out of the greater part of their glory. By trying to make the job seem fun and no-big-deal, the Navy may be repelling the people who want this kind of challenge.

Not everybody is looking for an easy, fun job.

{The Lady}

A friend of mine lives in a "haunted" house. It's a nice white farmhouse in the country, surrounded with gardens, and every few weeks he'll call in the middle of the night to say, "Someone is screaming in the basement. I'm going down with my gun, and if I don't call you back in five minutes, send the police!"

It's all very dramatic, but it's the kind of complaint that smells like a boast. It's the psychic equivalent of saying, "My diamond ring is *so very heavy*." Or, "I wish I could wear this thong bikini *without everyone lusting after me*."

My friend refers to his ghost as "the lady," and he complains about not getting any sleep because "the lady" was up all night, rattling pictures on the walls and resetting the clocks and thumping around the living room. He calls it "dancing." If he's tardy or upset, it's usually because of "the lady." She shouted his name outside the bedroom window all night, or turned the lights on and off.

This is a practical man who's never believed in ghosts. I'll call him "Patrick." Until he moved out to this farm, Patrick was like me: stable, practical, reasonable.

Now I think he's full of shit.

To prove this, I asked him to let me house-sit his farm while he was away on vacation. I needed the isolation and quiet to write, I told him. I promised to water the plants, and he went off and left me there for two weeks. Then I threw a little party.

This man, he's not my only deluded friend. Another friend—I'll call her "Brenda"—says she can see the future. Over dinner, she'll ruin your best story by suddenly drawing a huge gasp, covering her mouth with her hand, and rearing back in her chair with a look of wide-eyed terror on her face. When you ask what's wrong, she'll say, "Oh . . . nothing, really." Then close her eyes and try to shake the terrible vision from her mind.

When you persist, asking what's scared her, Brenda will lean over the table with tears in her eyes. She'll take your hand in hers and beg you, "Please, please. Just stay away from automobiles for the next six years."

For the next six years!

Brenda and Patrick, they're odd but they're my friends, always hungry for attention. "My ghost is too loud . . . I hate being able to see the future . . ."

For my little house party, I planned to invite Brenda and her psychic friends out to the haunted farmhouse. I planned to invite another group of stupid, ordinary friends who aren't troubled with any special extrasensory gifts. We'd drink red wine and watch the mediums flit around, lapsing into trances, channeling spirits, doing their automatic writing, levitating tables, while we laughed politely behind our hands.

So Patrick was gone on vacation. A dozen people arrived at the farmhouse. And Brenda brought two women I'd never met, Bonnie and Molly, both of them already swooning from the ghost energy they felt there. Every few steps, they stopped, swaying on their feet and grasping for a chair or railing to keep from falling to the floor. Okay, all my friends were swaying a little. But for the sane ones it was the red wine. We all sat around the dining room table, a couple lighted candles in the center, and the psychics went to work.

First they turned to my friend Ina. Ina's German and sensible. Her idea of expressing emotion is to light another cigarette. These mediums, Bonnie and Molly, they'd never met Ina before this moment, but they took turns telling her how a woman's spirit was beside her. The woman was named "Margaret" and was showering Ina with tiny blue flowers. Forget-me-nots, they said. And suddenly Ina put down her cigarette and started to cry.

Ina's mother had died of cancer several years earlier. Her mother's name was Margaret, and every year Ina sprinkled forget-me-not seeds on her grave because they'd been her mother's favorite flower. Ina and I have been friends for twenty years, and these are details even I didn't know. Ina never talks about her dead mother, and now she's weeping and asking for more red wine.

Having reduced my friend to a mess, Bonnie and Molly turned to me.

They said a man was near me, standing just over my shoulder. He was, they both agreed, my murdered father.

Oh, *please*. My father. Here, let's just take a little break from the nonsense.

Anyone could know the details of my father's death. The strange, ironic circle. When he was four years old, his own father had shot his mother, then stalked my father around the house, trying to shoot him. My dad's first memories are of hiding under a bed, hearing his father call and seeing his heavy boots walk past, the smoking barrel of the rifle hanging near the floor. While he hid, his father eventually shot himself. Then, my dad spent his life running from the scene. My siblings also say he spent his life trying to find his mother by marrying woman after woman. Always divorcing and remarrying. He'd been divorced from my mother for twenty years when he saw a personals advertisement in the newspaper. He started dating the author of the ad, not knowing she had a violent ex-husband. Coming home from their third date, they were surprised by the ex-husband, who shot them both in the woman's house. That was in April of 1999.

Really, these details have been published everywhere. The whole mess has gone to trial, and the murderer is sentenced to death. Bonnie and Molly needed no special gifts to know any of this.

But still they persisted. They said my father was very sorry for something he'd done to me when I was four years old. He knew it was cruel, but it was the only way he could think to teach me a lesson. He was a very young man at the time and didn't realize he was going too far. Bonnie and Molly, they held hands and said they saw me as a small boy, kneeling beside a chopping block. My father was standing over me, holding something wooden.

"It's a stick," they said, then, "No, it's not. It's an ax . . ."

The rest of my friends were quiet, Ina's weeping had shushed their giggling.

Bonnie and Molly said, "You're four years old, and you're

deciding something very important. It's something that will shape the rest of your life . . ."

They described my father sharpening his ax and said, "You're about to be . . ." they paused, then said, "dismembered?"

Ina's still over there sobbing. The silly cow. I pour another glass of wine and drink it. I pour another. I tell Bonnie and Molly, our guides to the ghost world, to please tell me more. I smirk and say, "No, really, this is fascinating."

Then they say, "Your father is very happy now. He's happier now than he ever was in his life on earth."

Oh, isn't that always the case? A little scrap of comfort for the bereaved. Bonnie and Molly are just the same sort who have preyed on grieving people throughout history. At best they're misguided, deluded fools. At worst, manipulative monsters.

What I don't tell them is, when I was four years old, I slipped a metal washer around my finger. It was too tight to remove, and I waited until my finger was swollen and purple before I asked my father for help. We'd always been told not to put rubber bands or anything tight around our fingers or we'd get gangrene and those bits would rot and fall off. My dad said we'd have to cut the finger off, and spent the afternoon washing my hand and sharpening the ax. The whole time, he also lectured me about taking responsibility for my own actions. He said that if I was going to do stupid things, I should be ready to pay the price.

That whole afternoon, I listened. There was no drama, no tears or panic. In my four-year-old mind, my father was doing me a favor. It would hurt, chopping off my fat, purple finger, but it would be better than the weeks of letting it rot.

I knelt beside the chopping block, where I'd seen so many chickens meet a similar fate, and put out my hand. If anything,

I was wildly grateful for my father's help, and resolved never to blame other people for stupid things I'd done.

My father swung the ax, and of course he missed. We went inside, and he used soap and water to remove the washer.

It's a story I'd almost forgotten. Almost forgotten, because I'd never told it to anyone, never re-remembered it by saying it aloud for anyone's reaction. Because I knew other people wouldn't understand the lesson. All they'd see is my father's actions and label it cruelty. God forbid telling my mother—she'd explode with righteous rage. Like my father's earliest memories of the shooting, that day with the ax is my oldest memory, and for thirty-six years it has been my secret. And my father's. And now these silly women, Bonnie and Molly, are telling it to me and all my drunken friends.

No way was I going to give them the satisfaction. While Ina sobbed, I drank more wine. I smiled and shrugged, saying it was all very interesting prattle, nevertheless it was nonsense. A few minutes later, one of the women fell to the floor, ill, and asked for help getting to her car. The party broke up, and Ina and I stayed behind to finish the wine and get blotto.

It was disappointing, really, that stupid party. Watching my friends take this nonsense so seriously. "The lady" never did appear, but Patrick will still call me to complain about his silly ghost problems. Brenda will still shudder and go pale before she announces her goofy premonitions. As far as Bonnie and Molly go, they were very lucky. It was a trick of some kind. Now everyone around me will stay just slightly deluded.

I can't explain Bonnie and Molly's little magic trick, but there's so much in the world I can't explain.

The night my father was killed, hundreds of miles away, my mother had a dream. She said my father knocked at her door, begging her to hide him. In her dream, he'd been shot in the side—later, the coroner would confirm this—and was trying to escape from a man with a gun. Instead of hiding him, my mother told him he'd brought nothing but shame and pain to his children, and she shut the door in his face.

That same night one of my sisters dreamt she was walking through the desert where we grew up. She was walking beside our father, telling him she was sorry they'd grown apart and not spoken recently. In her dream he stopped her and said the past didn't matter anymore. Our father told her he was very happy and she should be also.

That night he died, I didn't have any dream. No one came to me in my sleep to say goodbye.

A week later, the police called me to say they had a dead body and asked if I would come help identify it.

Oh, I'd love to believe in an invisible world. It would undermine all the suffering and pressure of the physical world. But it would also negate the value of the money I have in the bank, my decent house and all my hard work. All our problems and all our blessings could be readily dismissed because they'd be no more real than plot events in a book or movie. An invisible, eternal world would render this world an illusion.

Really, the spirit world is like pedophilia or necrophilia. I have no experience with it, so I am completely unable to take it seriously. It will always seem like a joke.

There are no ghosts.

But if there are, my dad should damn well tell me himself.

PORTRAITS

{In Her Own Words}

"One time," Juliette Lewis says, "I wanted to get to know someone better by writing down questions to him . . ." She says, "These questions are more telling about me than anything I could write in a diary."

Juliette says this on an antique sofa in a rented house in the Hollywood Hills, a very white and vertical, a very Getty Museum house—stark modern but full of her antique furniture—a house she's renting with her husband, Steve Berra, until they can move into their new home near Studio City. She's holding a handwritten list she's just found, and reads:

"Did you ever stab someone or cut them intentionally with a sharp object?"

She reads: "Do you like asparagus?"

She reads: "Do you have a middle name?"

She drinks chai. She doesn't watch television. She loves playing cards, King's Corner or Kings Around the Corner. She uses that fancy new toilet paper, Cottonelle, which feels like you're using a cashmere sweater. In the basement is Steve's severed head—a *very* realistic replica left over from a skateboard video and made by the same team that made Juliette's pregnant stomach for the movie *The Way of the Gun.*

From the list, Juliette reads: "Do cats frustrate you as pets, or do you admire their independence?"

Over the past twenty-four hours, she's talked about her family, her father (Geoffrey Lewis), her career, the Scientology thing, getting married, and writing songs. The songs are important because after years of being scripted, these are her words now.

Juliette's mother, Glenis Batley, says, "Okay, this is the great story."

This over breakfast in Los Angeles. Glenis drinks lots of coffee and has lots of red hair and is still the lovely woman who once modeled for an old photograph Juliette has framed at home.

Glenis says, "I got pregnant, and I was on this incredible diet that was absolutely pure, but I didn't really want anyone around. I noticed the contractions were five minutes apart so I called, and I got this one doctor that I didn't want, and he said that he'd be there right away. He said, 'Whatever you do, don't push.' So I went and I sort of reclined, and along comes the next contraction, and I get this irresistible urge to push, and I think, 'One little push won't hurt.' So she's born. And she's very *noisy*. Anyway, I'm holding this infant, and I nearly drop her, and now she's *really* sure that I don't know what I'm doing, so she's crying. And it's the first light of morning, and the doves are cooing, and up to then I hadn't known what her name was . . . Juliette!"

She says, "I decided to spell it the French way because the tragedy sucks."

From her list, Juliette reads: "Did you ever break a guy's nose?"

She reads: "Would you say you won more fights than you've lost?"

In her kitchen, grinding coffee beans, Juliette says, "When I was growing up, what influenced me were all these musicals. Like *Fame*. That was my dream. If I could have a school where they just sing and dance. So, *Fame* and *Flashdance* and *Grease*. Did you ever see the movie *Hair*? I was sobbing. That's a musical that kills me."

She says, "I was going to be a singer first. Before being an actress, I was going to sing. And I always thought I'd maybe act on the side. I always thought of musicals. Singing and dancing. I want to sing still, so I wrote songs with a friend who's a musician. The biggest fun thing is it's my words.

"The only break that I got was that my dad had me meet this small agency. Say hello. The big problem for actors starting out is getting *the agent*. Agents want you to have a SAG card, but you can't get your SAG card unless you have an agent putting you up for work. It's a catch-22. So my dad got me into an agent's office, but I still had to audition. I did a reading, and they had to see something in me.

"If you met me when I was younger, I was really quiet. I did a TV show once and people were asking my agent, 'Is she okay? She seems really down.' It was just your typical teenage crap.

Just because I don't smile at everyone and ask them how they're doing, I have to be sad?"

From her list, sitting on an antique sofa, Juliette reads: "Was there a time when you were mystified by the workings of your penis?"

She reads: "Do you look more like your mother or father?"

The tape recorder goes on and on, listening.

She says, "Even at eighteen I'd go, 'Where is the hidden rule book that says I *have to be made up?*' Because they'd have this chair and all this makeup. I was, like, 'Can't we just take a picture?' That's why all my magazines from earlier are not made up and they're not raw. They're in-between, and what shaped me is what they called the 'alternative girl' or the 'kookie girl' because I couldn't vamp up at the drop of a hat.

"When I was younger, they'd have a rack of clothing I'd never wear . . . They'd have a makeup person . . . And *I'm supposed to represent myself?* It was like this weird thing. I'd always wanted to be like my male predecessors, like Brando or De Niro. You take a man, and you just document him in a picture.

"What you exude, your sexuality is just a part of oneself. So a manufactured sex appeal which includes an open mouth and lip gloss and bright colors, this is this American porn sex appeal which has nothing to do with sex. It's like blowup dolls. I could *do* that, very easily. It's not like I can't. It's just never been my objective.

"Now I realize you're selling things," Juliette says. "So you basically become a rack."

She reads: "Did you date an older woman that you'd consider an older woman, and what did she teach you?"

"What's the first image you have of the female body?"

She asks: "Does the respect factor drop when a woman has breast implants?"

Juliette says, "I had two dreams about De Niro when I was working with him. I think it was all in anticipation of this scene. Because this, in my head, was *the big scene*. In one dream, we were underwater in a pool and we'd come up for air. He'd go underwater, and I'd go underwater, and we'd glide past each other deliberately, like kids would play in a pool when they like each other. Like a flirtation. But I woke up from that dream, and I had a crush on him.

"In that scene, the little tango dance between our characters, all I knew was he was supposed to walk up to me, and then say, 'Danielle, can I put my arm around you?' He's supposed to kiss me in the script, but all Scorsese said was, 'Bob's going to do something. Just go with the scene.'

"Before that scene, I knew we were going to film the kiss part. I had just eaten lunch. It was catfish or something, and I was, like, 'Should I rinse my mouth out?' But I didn't want to, because that would let him know I *thought* about it. I don't want to act like I thought about the kiss. You're damned if you do and damned if you don't. So I didn't. I didn't do mouthwash. And then I get to the set, and Bob is right near me, and I smell *mouthwash*. And then it dawned on me in that moment— I felt like such a little kid—because I thought, 'He's being professional. He's being considerate of me. He's being courteous.' But by then it was too late to go back to the trailer. I don't know if I was offensive or not.

"When you watch it, that's the first take. We did it twice. He puts the thumb on my lips. It's very intense because we're only *this* far from each other, and I'm looking right at him. He starts to put the thumb in my mouth, and she moves it away. And then he persists, and she allows it. And people after that kept talking about the sexuality and burgeoning sexuality at that age, and I never looked at it that way. I looked at it as, before he did the thumb thing he was *listening* to her, he was validating her in a way that her parents weren't, and then he did this sexual thing. But what you see in my eyes is, after she sucks the thumb and it gets pulled out, she's looking at him like, 'Was that *good*? Did you like that?' It's a pleasing thing."

She says, "His thumb was very *clean*."

She reads: "Did you go to sleep-away summer camp? (Because some of my greatest childhood memories are from summer camp.)"

She reads: "Do you like roller coasters?"

Steve Berra says, "A long time ago, I was on tour, skateboarding, and I bought *Kalifornia* at this gas station. I remember trying to imitate a laugh that she did in one of her scenes. It had blown me away. Just this one little laugh the character Adele did. It was so natural and truthful, and I remember trying for ten minutes to laugh however she did it. I didn't know her. I couldn't figure out how the hell this person was so good."

A video copy of the movie is playing in their living room, and Juliette laughs, pointing out all the lines she just ad-libbed in the moment.

Juliette says, "On the page, my little character, Adele, had maybe a sentence here and there in a scene. So I met with Dominic Sena and was really taken with his energy and his vision for the movie. He was very enthusiastic. So basically he let me create that character. Ninety percent of what I do in that movie I made up there. That was like a turning point for me, acting-wise, because I had to really come to the table with something, really invent something. To me, my first official character. That little Adele character."

She reads: "What do you imagine happens to someone after the body dies? And do you believe that you are a spirit with a body or just a brain?"

Then, "The follow-up question is: How do you explain Mozart writing symphonies at seven? (Because I think that's a prime example of creative ability being spirit-generated.)"

Juliette says, "When you have good actors to work with, you guys just sort of create this alternate universe of pretended reality. It's the unexplainable. I just think it's magic. It's pure belief. My security blanket is the camera. I know the camera's universe. It's capturing only *this much*. I have a certain security or certainty that I can execute stuff in that space. It's the condensed reality of the camera.

"Sometimes, you want to put in an aside that goes, 'By the way, audience, it was really three in the morning when we did this scene. It was thirty degrees outside. And I brought you all of this despite all of that.' It was *That Night*, a movie I did before *Cape Fear* had come out. It was this 1962 love story. A guy from the wrong side of the tracks. Very endearing, very sweet. I was supposed to meet him in the middle of the night on a pier in Atlantic City. It was freezing, but it was supposed to be summer. You know, those hot nights. Meanwhile, I'm kind of blue. My lips go, 'brrrrrr,' and they chatter. So I had to hold it so I'm not chattering, plus be in a summer dress. You'd be in your parka until they said, 'Okay, we're ready for you.' Then you'd take it off and say, 'Gosh, I'm so in love . . .'

"When I worked on *From Dusk Till Dawn*, the vampire

movie when I worked with George Clooney, he said, 'Gosh, all my friends keep asking, "Ooo, so you're working with Juliette. Is she really psycho? Is she really intense?"' And I'm like the most opposite from intense. Maybe when I was young I was a bit brooding. Maybe I'll cop to that. My work is actually, really a light process. I go in and out of it. When the camera's going, I'm on. When it's off, I'm off."

She says, "When people want to know how you're able to do what you do, they need to explain it. It helps them if they go, 'Okay so you're kind of really crazy, and that's how you're able to be really intense onscreen.' They need an explanation, when my explanation is, it's magic."

From her list, she reads: "Did the female anatomy ever mystify and scare you? (Because it did me, and I'm the owner.)"

Driving past the Scientology Celebrity Centre, she says, "The whole thing in Scientology, the big motto is: What's real for you is real for you. So there's not, like, a dogma. It's simply an applied religious philosophy. And there's little courses, like the Success Through Communications Course. They have things you can apply to your life, but not like a falsity, not like a robot-thing. You can see if it works, and if it doesn't. If it works, it works. It's something that has helped me a great deal."

From the list, she reads: "Have you ever been caught in a natural disaster?"

She reads: "Did you ever own Birkenstocks?"

Just outside her bedroom door, looking at a framed, poster-sized picture of herself and Woody Harrelson from the cover of *Newsweek*, Juliette says, "With *Natural Born Killers*, I've appreciated as times goes by how that movie is satire and my character is a caricature, although I filled it with some real human emotion. But to me it's kind of campy. It's silly. It's exaggerated beyond what's real. I just had to give it some energy, like that whole beginning sequence—*how sexy am I now!*—where she's yelling. I have a big voice, so I can turn the volume up, but when we'd cut, it felt silly. Everyone thought, ooooh, I must've been so disturbed, but I wasn't. To me it was just very campy, that performance."

About how people reacted to the movie, Juliette says, "You could homogenize everything, but you're still going to have your exploders, your guys who explode. And why is that there? I think since the fifties, the increase in psychiatric drugs has turned that into a landslide from what it was . . . I did research. I actually spoke at some Senate meetings, but that would be a much bigger problem for them to deal with, considering that you have six million kids from six on up on Ritalin. So they don't even want to look at it. They'd rather just say, 'Could you guys just please be less violent in the movies?'

"Here you have the famous Son of Sam guy, the killer, he said why he killed was the dog barking was giving him messages. Was the Devil speaking through the dog. Okay, so do we lock up all dogs? Because of what that criminal says?"

From her list, she reads: "What was your favorite expression growing up? Or what was it closer to:

> That's so fresh.
> That's so bitchin'.
> That's so wicked.
> That's so rad.
> Or, that's so hot."

Juliette says, "I don't think you have to use your past to create in the present. There's different schools of acting where you have an incident that was painful and you match it up to the movie and use it. To me that's too complicated. I just surrender to the material. I just have to surrender.

"To me, the three hardest things to do in acting are: one, sobbing, because I so rarely do that in my life. I may well up, but I don't sob. Laughing hysterically is another, where it says 'She can't stop laughing.' And the third one is being surprised or being scared, like, 'Gosh, you scared me!' You have to think backward, like, 'When I get scared, what happens?' Oh, maybe my hands shake after the initial shock. It takes a minute to get your breath back. You work on getting to that place.

"To sob, I usually use the pressure or the fear that I have to do it, and if I don't do it, I'll fail. I'll fail myself. I'll fail my director. I'll fail the movie. People have this faith in me to produce. The frustration that I *can't* cry will lead me to tears."

She says, "I was doing *Natural Born Killers*, with Oliver Stone, and it was this scene with Woody Harrelson up on a hill, and we're arguing. And I'd just gotten my period that morning, and didn't sleep very well. I'd gotten about an hour's sleep, plus the pain of the *woman thing*, and we're arguing, and we cut.

"Woody's like, 'You want to do it again? I want to do another take.'

"And Oliver's like, 'Yeah. How about you, Juliette? You want to do it again?'

"And I go, 'Why? It sucks. What's the point? I suck. I don't even know why I'm doing this. I'm not going to get any better! It sucks! It's terrible!'

"And they look at me, and Oliver says, he pulls me aside and says, 'Juliette, nobody wants to hear how you suck. Nobody here cares that you think you suck.' And from that point, I stopped doing that. It was such a turning point. Such a very good thing he did. He stopped me from catering to that little shit."

She reads: "Did you ever fall in love with an animal in a way where you wished you could talk like human friends? (Because I would fall in love with my cats and wish that we were the same species so we could relate.)"

At a party in Westwood, actress and screenwriter Marissa Ribisi watches Juliette and Steve eating chicken and says, "They're so cute together. They're like a couple dudes."

Leaving the party, under a full moon, they take fortune cookies and get the same fortune: "Avenues of Good Fortune Are Ahead for You."

Driving home from the party, Juliette says, "All I thought about for a wedding was to have a view. We were outside on a cliff. It was the first time I saw him in a suit, and he was dashing. My view—because I had to walk this little trail that came out of this tunnel, because there was this park, then a tunnel, then this cliff—and as I was getting closer it was just this silhouette of this man with the sun behind him. It was incredible."

She says, "I kept thinking, 'Should I have the veil down or veil up? Veil down? Veil up?' I loved the idea of a veil, because inside it's like a dream. And that's what wedding days are like."

Steve says, "I didn't have shoes. All I had time to do was buy a suit so I didn't have shoes that would go with it. So I had to borrow my friend's shoes. We just swapped them on the cliff. For the pictures."

The VCR in their living room breaks, so they're watching Steve's skateboard videos on the bedroom television, and Juliette says, "When I first saw his skateboarding videos, I welled up in tears. First of all, the music is so beautiful, and he chose the music, the piano. It is so aesthetic to me, his gliding and jumping and defying the physical universe. Because that's not supposed to be done. You don't take an object with wheels, and jump off a structure. It's a defiance. It was the first time I was able to be awed by a partner in this way."

Upstairs, looking at a framed photo of Marilyn Monroe, Juliette says, "People have reduced Marilyn to a sex symbol, but the reason she had so much power is she made people light up. She had a joy. When she's smiling in a picture, she's a blend. She's in a female body, this beautiful woman form, but she has that child-love shining through, this kind of child-light that makes other people light up, too. I think that's what's special about her.

"There's a word for it in Scientology. What's common to children is they give off . . . how they're able to uplift, their joy, it's called '*theta*.' It's what's innate to a spirit. So in Scientology, a spirit is called a thetan, and what a spirit would give off is theta. It's what I would call *magic*."

Reading from her list of questions left over from that long-ago romance, she says: "Do you feel that we are all potentially Christlike?"

She says: "Do you have hope for humanity? And if not, how

can you honestly keep on going in the face of that hopelessness?"

She stresses, "There are no right answers to these."

POSTSCRIPT: Halfway to Juliette's house, the man who was driving me got a call. Apparently the magazine's credit card wouldn't authorize payment, and the dispatcher told the driver to "obtain payment from the passenger." Payment for half a day's driving was about $700. The week before this, a hotel gave me the same story about another magazine's credit card, then billed both my credit card and the magazine's. I felt pretty cagey about the double-billing issue, and told him no way. He told me I was a thief. I told him to let me out at the next stoplight. He locked the doors and said, no, and my bag was still in the trunk. I started calling the magazine in New York, but by then everyone had gone home. For the next two hours, we drove around the Hollywood Hills with the doors locked, the driver shouting that I was responsible. I was a thief. I shouldn't use a service I can't pay for.

I'm telling him how the magazine made all the arrangements. And I keep calling New York. Still, I'm thinking, *Wow, I'm a limo hostage. This is so cool!*

Eventually, I call 911 and say I'm being kidnapped. A minute later the driver throws me and my bag out in the gutter in front of Juliette's house.

I never told her what happened. I just went up and rang the doorbell. She and Steve probably still think I'm always this shaky, sweaty mess.

Turns out the magazine's credit card was just fine . . .

{Why Isn't He Budging?}

"I [Andrew Sullivan] was born in 1963 in a small, actually *very* small town in southern England, grew up in another small town not far away in southern England, got a scholarship to Oxford, then I went and got *another* scholarship to go to grad school in Harvard in '84, and did a public administration degree at the Kennedy School and then realized that I couldn't cope with the sort of regression analysis of welfare reform and moved into philosophy, mainly political philosophy, and then did a Ph.D. in political science, mainly political theory, in the next few years, and while I was doing that I sort of moonlighted by going down to Washington and interning at the *New Republic*, and then going back and being a junior editor and then becoming editor of the *New Republic*, I guess, in 1991, and doing that through '96, and then putting an end to that and sort of getting my life together."

"I had a . . . I hated my family life. I hated it. I had a very visceral hostility to the circumstances in which I found myself growing up, and I think I detached quite early . . . I didn't enjoy it when my parents were fighting at all. I was horrified and traumatized by it . . . To some extent you get used to it. My mother was incredibly frank and direct about everything, and it was all very—raw. My father was always slamming doors and yelling and screaming and getting drunk and playing rugby, and my mother was always complaining and yelling. I mean, this was on and on and on, and I think a part of me just sort of withdrew from all of that and saw it as a spectator sport, but part of me was also extremely traumatized by it. But whether you're traumatized or not, it's where you're at home. Even if it's a horrible trauma, this is what the therapists tell you, and I think it makes a lot of sense. Even if it's deep unhappiness, it's *your* unhappiness."

"Well, maybe that does follow that one seeks out relationships that replicate that . . ."

"I was confirmed in Arundel Cathedral in Sussex. I come from Sussex. My family doesn't. They come from some bog in Ireland somewhere. But Sussex was a very English Catholic county and many English martyrs came from there and that was part of my identity as a kid."

"My confirmation saint was Saint Thomas More . . . I was an English Catholic boy, and I guess it was a way of affirming a particular kind of identity and resistance to England, to all of its anti-Catholic trappings, and also More has always completely fascinated me. He's an intensely fascinating man for all the obvious reasons, the attempt to be in the world/not be in the world. Be knee-deep in politics. Be even deeper into his spiritual life. He brings together all sorts of questions about what integrity is, loyalty."

"The one area that really interests me is sanctity. I'm interested in what saints are. Because it's . . . I don't know what they are, and I should, really. I think we all should have a better grip on what that's all about, what a human being who is a human being and yet somehow holy, somehow in touch with something else more profoundly than anybody else . . . And there are several saints that sort of fascinate me, and I would love to figure out some more about. Saint Francis is one. Saint John the Beloved is another . . ."

"There's something appealing about the figure who—and I'm sure I sort of project onto this on some level—who's standing by himself. Who's just there and won't budge. You ask yourself, 'Why isn't he budging? What's going on? Why? Why? Why?' "

"I used to be envious of people who were positive [for HIV]. Because I felt like they were living in some enhanced way that I had not yet been able to achieve. This is where sanctity comes in. The whole definition of a saint is somebody who lives as if they're going to die tonight. A saint is so in touch with reality, which is of course our mortality, that he's able to live at a different level of intensity . . . I found myself falling in love with people who were positive . . . A couple people I'm thinking of,

I think they really were quite remarkable in how they tackled their disease and lived with it and overcame it and shone with it even as they died. There is something particularly attractive about it, just as we're attracted to martyrs, and we're fascinated by suicide bombers . . . None of those people wanted to be in the situation they were in, but they had a certain impatience with stupidity and ephemera."

"Without getting into any details, I've just had this very very *very* tempestuous and short-lived relationship that I bumped into in San Francisco. I just bumped into him on Saturday night . . . Our last contact was just sort of a very peremptory and vicious email, and I saw him and talked to him and we didn't raise our voices or anything. We were talking, and my friends pointed out that they noticed two things. One, they noticed that obviously we were angry but that there was an incredible intensity about the relationship.

"There was something between the two of us that just crackled when we were together. And I guess I *do* like that. It keeps me from being bored."

"Being married doesn't mean you're less alone. I think a relationship can be the most intense form of being alone if you're not careful . . . Friendship is what really resolves and mitigates loneliness while not compromising the self in the way that love does, romantic love does. And More was not completely alone. He had his daughter, who was very close to him, and he had some wonderful friends."

"That's a big question: 'Why are you alone?' I mean, we're all alone. Aloneness is . . . that's life. It's the quality of our aloneness that matters. Whether it's quality solitude. I am a solitary person. I always have been, ever since I was a kid. I guess it's hard . . . it takes a lot for me to let somebody in."

"Someone once pointed out: 'Among straight people, you're a gay guy. Among English people, you're a Catholic. An Irish Catholic. Among Americans, you're sort of English. Among the academia establishment, you're a hack. Among the hacks, you're a sort of academic. You keep displacing yourself out of any particular team.' "

"It might be a defensive response. I mean, the Republicans don't want anything to do with me. Neither do the Democrats. People on the right are very suspicious of me. So are people on the left . . . I like to think that I try to think and write for myself, and sometimes that means that you do piss off people, on a regular basis. Solitude is a natural place for a writer to be. And, again, it's not like my models . . . like Orwell was the hero of any group of people, I mean, he was very much on his own. I'm very leery of attachment."

"It's terrible, the minute I feel like everybody agrees with me, I want to change my mind. I'm such a sort of—and this is probably why I was not very good at the management side of being an editor—because I was literally more comfortable in opposition to my entire staff than sort of gently uniting them. Or even our readership [of the *New Republic*], I always kept people, I tried to keep everybody on edge.

"Obviously I've thought about this to some extent. I don't want to problemitize it in some ways. I think it's how you are, but . . . it's what makes me feel secure, I think, that lack of security."

"I'm not interested in being well received or not well received. When you start thinking like that, you're finished, I think. The only interesting question for me is whether I can convey certain things I'm trying to convey more effectively through the medium of fictional narrative than through trying to write stuff that is argumentative. You know, right now, out there there's either factual stuff, biographical, historical stuff, or there's fiction. The genre of political or moral writing for anybody to read is really slim, which isn't purely sort of temporary political I'm-right/they're-wrong kind of Jim Carville stuff."

"*Virtually Normal* was a weird book in the sense that—*I* don't think of it as a weird book—but it was an attempt to say that an issue like this, which is so mired in emotion and psychology, could be written about in a classical rationalist fashion. Its model, that book, was the sort of nineteenth-century polemicists and pamphleteers I sort of admired—not too long, and anybody could read it and generate a discussion, and those sort of pamphlets in the late nineteenth century were wonderful things."

"[*Virtually Normal*] came out in '95, so I wrote it in '94 while I was still editor, and I did a sort of prototype of the argument in an essay in the *New Republic* in '93 ['The Politics of Homosexuality']. And meanwhile I wrote about a lot of other things and kept writing a kind of American commentary for British papers, which eventually I got a good deal with, and write for the *Times*, and sort of carved out a way of paying the rent that way. But subsequent to leaving the *New Republic*, I've sort of moved out of editing and I'm concentrating more on writing."

"It wasn't quite drama, but it was energy. I don't think it was manufactured drama. It was energy. And I had that sort of interaction with my fellow editors, too . . . It was just a tempestuous place. A lot of big people with strong ideas butting heads. I mean, that's the nature of those sort of places. They attract people like me, and people like me don't get along with people like me."

". . . To begin with, that's what I wanted to be when I was a kid. It's where I thought I was going to go, elective politics . . . I think that I *do* do that in part. I think that politics is what you make it . . . I go around the country and I speak. I go from high schools to political rallies. I'll speak at big fund raisers, and I do all that stuff all the time . . . It's interesting, but I think that what I'm trying to do is both a forensic thing—to simply dissect and point out the inadequacy of the argument on the other side, whether you're against Jerry Falwell or Pat Buchanan or whoever—and, secondly, you're doing, you're performing an exemplary role, you're saying, 'I'm also a gay person and I'm here.' That very fact changes the debate we're talking about, precisely because part of what we're talking about is shame, and the capacity to resist shame and overcome it. And that is something that cannot be argued. It has to be shown. It has to be felt by people who see it for them to absorb it, and grow from it, and do it themselves. And I feel that half the time that's also what I'm doing. That I achieve ninety-five percent of what I'm doing merely by showing up. You look at them straight in the eyes . . . It's funny, but I was on *Politically Incorrect* with Lou Sheldon last week, and he said, 'I don't think it's a disease. It's a dysfunction'—talking about homosexuality—and all I did was say, 'Hey, I'm here. Stop talking about me as if I don't exist' . . . You can't talk about us in the same way anymore, because we're here. You have to take us seriously."

"I don't know what my role should be. I've struggled with it. You'd be amazed, the hostility I still get thrown at me . . . I think as soon as I held a position I'd be completely demolished by the people I'm supposed to represent . . . It's a very tough world out there . . . There is extreme resistance to that sort of leadership in the gay and lesbian world. It's a very fractious place . . . I hate to sound so vague and confused, but I don't know. I think we're feeling our way. I'm feeling my way."

"I'm scared of a relapse into not believing in ourselves, a relapse into thinking of ourselves as irrelevancies or shallow things, people that don't need full emotional lives, don't need full political lives—that this could return. I'm not a Whig. I don't think these things are inevitable. I think they're choices, which is why I was so keen to see marriage at least as a residue, some sort of tangible legacy of AIDS, and we haven't got it. The Hawaii result and the Alaska result show that we have so much more work to do in talking to straight people to persuade them that this is reality and that we need it and that we deserve it. And so much more to do in telling *ourselves* that we deserve it. And *believing* that we deserve it. But it's hard. It's extremely hard."

"In many ways I do feel like this book [*Love Undetected*] is a real attempt to draw a line under a certain part of my life and try and move on. And I didn't feel I could do that without writing it, so it had a sort of purgative effect. It probably comes across like that, too. It came up like puke. Even the abstract stuff came out like puke. It got to the point where I realized I wasn't going to finish it because I had nothing to say about friendship, for example, then I just [makes puking noise], in two weeks wrote that last thing. Just three to four hours per day just speed-writing."

"You get to a point on these things where I just need to sleep for a long time and wake up and get my life back together again before I can figure out what you write next."

"I feel like I'm saying things here that I shouldn't say. I guess it doesn't matter."

{Not Chasing Amy}

When you study minimalism in Tom Spanbauer's workshop, the first story you read is Amy Hempel's "The Harvest." Next you read Mark Richard's story "Strays." After that, you're ruined.

If you love books, if you love to read, this is a line you may not want to cross.

I'm not kidding. You go beyond this point, and almost every book you'll ever read will suck. All those thick, third-person, plot-driven books torn from the pages of today's news, well, after Amy Hempel, you'll save yourself a lot of time and money.

Or not. Every year on the itemized Schedule C of my tax return, I deduct more money for new copies of Hempel's three books, *Reasons to Live*, *At the Gates of the Animal Kingdom*, and *Tumble Home*. Every year, you want to share these books. What happens is they never come back. Good books never do. This is why my office shelves are crowded with nonfiction too gross for most people, mostly forensic autopsy textbooks, and a ton of novels I hate.

At a bar in New York last year, the literary bar KGB in the East Village, Hempel told me her first book is out of print. The only copy I know of is behind glass in the Powell's rare book room, a first-edition hardcover selling for $75, without a signature.

I have a rule about meeting the flesh-and-blood version of people whose work I love. That rule I'm saving for the end.

Unless Hempel's books are reprinted, I may end up spending more, or making fewer friends. You cannot *not* push these books on people, saying, "Read this," saying, "Is it just me, or did it make you cry, too?"

I once gave *Animal Kingdom* to a friend and said, "If you don't love this, we have nothing in common."

Every sentence isn't crafted, it's *tortured* over. Every quote and joke, what Hempel tosses out comedian-style, is something funny or profound enough you'll remember it for years. The same way, I sense, Hempel has remembered it, held on to it, saved it for a place where it could really shine. Scary jewelry metaphor, but her stories are studded and set with these compelling bits. Chocolate-chip cookies with no bland cookie "matrix," just nothing but chips and chopped walnuts.

In that way, her experience becomes your experience. Teachers talk about how students need to have an emotional breakthrough, an "ah-hah!" discovery moment in order to retain information. Fran Lebowitz still writes about the moment she first looked at a clock and grasped the concept of telling time.

Hempel's work is nothing but these flashes, and every flash makes you ache with recognition.

Right now, Tom Spanbauer's teaching another batch of students by photocopying "The Harvest" from his old copy of *The Quarterly*, the magazine edited by Gordon Lish, the man who taught minimalism to Spanbauer and Hempel and Richard. And, through Tom, to me.

At first, "The Harvest" looks like a laundry list of details. You have no idea why you're almost weeping by the end of seven pages. You're a little confused and disoriented. It's just a simple list of facts presented in the first person, but somehow it adds up to more than the sum of its parts. Most of the facts are funny as hell, but at the last moment, when you're disarmed by laughter, it breaks your heart.

She breaks your heart. First and foremost. That evil Amy Hempel. That's the first bit Tom teaches you. A good story should make you laugh, and a moment later break your heart. The last bit is *you will never write this well*. You won't learn this part until you've ruined a lot of paper, wasting your free time with a pen in one hand for years and years. At any horrible moment, you might pick up a copy of Amy Hempel and find your best work is just a cheap rip-off of her worst.

To demonstrate minimalism, students sit around Spanbauer's kitchen table for ten weeks taking apart "The Harvest."

The first aspect you study is what Tom calls "horses." The metaphor is—if you drive a wagon from Utah to California, you use the same horses the whole way. Substitute the word "themes" or "choruses" and you get the idea. In minimalism, a story is a symphony, building and building, but never losing the original melody line. All characters and scenes, things that seem dissimilar, they all illustrate some aspect of the story's theme. In "The Harvest," we see how every detail is some aspect of mortality and dissolution, from kidney donors to stiff fingers to the television series *Dynasty*.

The next aspect Tom calls "burnt tongue." A way of saying something, but saying it wrong, twisting it to slow down the reader. Force the reader to read close, maybe read twice, not just skim along a surface of abstract images, short-cut adverbs, and clichés.

In minimalism, clichés are called "received text."

In "The Harvest" Hempel writes: "I moved through the days like a severed head that finishes a sentence." Right here, you have her "horses" of death and dissolution *and* her writing a sentence that slows you to a more deliberate, attentive speed.

Oh, and in minimalism, no abstracts. No silly adverbs like "sleepily," "irritably," "sadly," please. And no measurements, no feet, yards, degrees, or years old. The phrase "an eighteen-year-old girl," what does *that* mean?

In "The Harvest," Hempel writes: "The year I began to say *vahz* instead of *vase*, a man I barely knew nearly accidentally killed me."

Instead of some dry age or measurement, we get the image of someone just becoming sophisticated, plus there's burnt tongue, plus she uses her "horse" of mortality.

See how these things add up?

What else you learn about minimalism includes "recording angel." This means writing without passing judgment. Nothing is fed to the reader as "fat" or "happy." You can only describe actions and appearances in a way that makes a judgment occur in the reader's mind. Whatever it is, you unpack it into the details that will reassemble themselves within the reader.

Amy Hempel does this. Instead of telling us the boyfriend in "The Harvest" is an asshole, we see him holding a sweater soaked with his girlfriend's blood and telling her, "You'll be okay, but this sweater is ruined."

Less becomes more. Instead of the usual flood of general details, you get a slow drip of single-sentence paragraphs, each one evoking its own emotional reaction. At best, she's a lawyer who presents her case, exhibit by exhibit. One piece of evidence at a time. At worst, she's a magician, tricking people. But reading, you always take the bullet without being told it's coming.

So, we've covered "horses" and "burnt tongue" and "recording angel." Now, writing "on the body."

Hempel shows how a story doesn't have to be some constant stream of blah-blah-blah to bully the reader into paying attention. You don't have to hold the reader by both ears and ram every moment down their throat. Instead, story can be a succession of tasty, smelly, touchable details. What Tom Spanbauer and Gordon Lish call "going on the body," to give the reader a sympathetic physical reaction, to involve the reader on a gut level.

The only problem with Hempel's palace of fragments is quoting it. Take any piece out of context, and it loses power. The French philosopher Jacques Derrida likens writing fiction to a software code that operates in the hardware of your mind. Stringing together separate macros that, combined, will create a reaction. No fiction does this as well as Hempel's, but each story is so tight, so boiled to bare facts, that all you can do is lie on the floor, face down, and praise it.

My rule about meeting people is—if I love their work, I don't want to risk seeing them fart or pick their teeth. Last summer in New York I did a reading at the Barnes & Noble on Union Square where I praised Hempel, telling the crowd that if she wrote enough, I'd just stay home and read in bed all day. The next night, she appeared at my reading in the Village. I drank half a beer and we talked without passing gas.

Still, I kind of hope I never see her again. But I did buy that first edition for $75.

{Reading Yourself}

It's almost midnight in Marilyn Manson's attic.

This is at the top of a spiral staircase where the skeleton of a seven-foot-tall man, the bones black with age, crouches, his human skull replaced by a ram's skull. He's the altarpiece from an old Satanic church in Britain, Manson says. Next to the skeleton is the artificial leg a man pulled off himself and gave to Manson after a concert. Next to that is the mullet wig from the movie *Joe Dirt*.

This is at the end of ten years' work. It's a new start. The alpha and the omega for this man who's worked a decade to become the most despised, the most frightening artist in music. As a coping skill. A defense mechanism. Or just out of boredom.

The walls are red, and as Manson sits on the black carpet, shuffling Tarot cards, he says, "It's hard to read yourself."

Somewhere, he says, he's got the skeleton of a seven-year-old Chinese boy, disassembled and sealed in plastic bags.

"I think I might make a chandelier out of it," he says.

Somewhere is the bottle of absinthe he drinks despite the fear of brain damage.

Here in the attic are his paintings and the working manuscript for his new book, a novel. He brings out the designs for a new deck of Tarot cards. It's him on almost every card. Manson as the Emperor, sitting in a wheelchair with prosthetic legs, clutching a rifle, with the American flag hung upside down behind him. Manson as the headless Fool, stepping off a cliff with grainy images of Jackie O in her pink suit and a JFK campaign poster in the background.

"It was a matter of reinterpreting the Tarot," he says. "I replaced the swords with guns. And Justice is weighing the Bible against the Brain."

He says, "Because each card has so many different symbols, there is a real magic, ritual element to it. When you shuffle, you're supposed to transfer your energy to the cards. It sounds kind of hokey. It's not something I do all the time. I like the symbolism much more than the trying to rely on divination.

"I think a reasonable question would be, 'What's next?'" he says, about to deal the cards and begin his reading. "More specific, 'What's my next step?'"

Manson deals his first card: the Hierophant

"The first card that you put down," Manson says, looking at the upside-down card, "this represents wisdom and forethought, and the fact that I just dealt it upside down could mean the opposite—like a lack. I could be naive about something. This card is, right now, my direct influence."

This reading takes place after Rose McGowen's left the house they share in the Hollywood Hills. After Manson and McGowen played with their Boston terriers, Bug and Fester, and she showed him a catalogue with the Halloween costumes she wants to order for the dogs. She talks about the "Boston Tea Party," where hundreds of people parade their Boston terriers around an L.A. park. They talk about how they rented a 1975 powder-blue Cadillac limo—the only rental available—to drive out to some snow-bound farm in the Midwest where they bought two of the terriers for Manson's parents.

Her car and driver are outside, waiting. She's catching a red-eye flight to Canada, where she's making a movie with Alan Alda. In the kitchen, a monitor shows views from the different security cameras, and McGowen talks about how different Alan Alda looks, how big his nose is. Manson tells her how, as men grow older, their nose and ears and scrotum keep growing. His mom, a nurse, talked about old men whose balls hung halfway down their legs.

Manson and McGowen kiss goodbye.

"Thanks a lot," she says. "Now when I work with Alan Alda, I'll be wondering how big his scrotum is."

In the attic, Manson deals his second card: Justice

"This could be referring to my judgment," he says, "my ability to discern, possibly with friendships or business dealings. Right now this is representing where I'm at. I feel a little naive or unsure about either friendships or business dealings, which does particularly apply to certain circumstances between me and my record company. So that makes every bit of sense."

The day before, in the offices of his record label on Santa Monica Boulevard, Manson sat on a black leather sofa, wearing black leather pants, and whenever he shifted, the leather-on-leather made a deep growl sound, amazingly similar to his voice.

"I tried to swim when I was a kid, but I could never deal with the water in my nose. I have a fear of the water. I don't like the ocean. There's something too infinite about it that I find dangerous."

The walls are dark blue and there are no lights on. Manson sits in this dark-blue room with the air conditioning blasting, drinking cola and wearing sunglasses.

"I guess I have a tendency to like to live in places where I don't really fit. I started out in Florida, and maybe that made me not fit. That was the thing that drove me to like and be attracted to everything opposite of my surroundings, because I didn't like the beach culture."

He says, "I used to just like to look. When I didn't know anybody and I first moved to Florida, I'd sit and I'd watch people. Just listen to conversations and observe. If you intend to create something that people will observe and listen to, you've got to listen to them first. That's the key to it."

At home, in the attic of his five-story house, drinking a glass of red wine, Manson deals his third card: the Fool

"The third card is to represent my goals," he says, the leather-rubbing-leather sound in his voice. "The Fool is about to walk off of a cliff, and it's a good card. It represents embarking on a journey, or taking a big step forward. That could represent the campaign of the record coming out or going on tour now."

He says, "I have a fear of crowded rooms. I don't like being around a lot of people, but I feel very comfortable onstage in front of thousands of people. I think it's a way of dealing with that."

His voice is so deep and soft, it disappears behind the rush of the air conditioning.

"I am very shy, strangely enough," he says, "and that's the irony of being an exhibitionist, being up in front of people. I'm really very shy.

"I like to sing alone, too. The least amount of people are involved whenever I'm singing. When I'm recording, sometimes I'll make them hit *record* and leave the room."

About touring, he says, "The threat of death makes it all worth living, makes it all exciting. That's the ultimate relief of boredom. Being right in the middle of it all. I thought, 'I know that I'm going to have to take things to such an extreme to get my points across that I'm going to start at the bottom and make myself the most despised person. I'm going to represent everything that you're against and you can't say anything to hurt me, to make me feel any worse. I only have *up* to go.' I think that was the most rewarding, to feel like there's nothing you can do to hurt me. Aside from killing me. Because I represent the bottom. I'm the worst that it gets, so you can't say that I did something that makes me look bad, because I'm telling you right now that I'm all of it. It was very liberating to not have to worry about how people are going to try and knock you down.

"If you don't like my music, I don't care. It doesn't really matter to me. If you don't like what I look like, if you don't like what I have to say, it's all part of what I'm asking for. You're giving me just what I want."

————

Manson deals his fourth card: Death

"The fourth card is your distant past," he says. "And the Death card most represents transition, and it's part of what has got you to this, how you are right now. This makes a good deal of sense, regarding the fact that I've just gone through such a grand transition that's taken place over the course of the last ten years."

Sitting in the dark-blue room at his record label, he says, "I think that my mom has in some ways that Munchausen syndrome, when people try and convince you that you're ill so they can hang on to you longer. Because when I was young, my mom used to always tell me I was allergic to different things that I'm not allergic to. She used to tell me I'm allergic to eggs and fabric softener and all kind of weird things. That's part of the medical element, too, because my mom's a nurse."

His black leather pants flare to cover thick-soled black shoes.

He says, "I remember that my urethra had grown closed, and they had to put a drill in my dick and drill it out. It was the worst thing that could ever happen to a kid. They told me that after I went through puberty I had to come back and go through it again, but I said, 'No chance. I don't care what my urine stream is like now. I'm not going back.'"

His mother still keeps his foreskin in a vial.

"When I was growing up, my dad and I didn't get along. He was never around, and that's why I didn't really talk about him, because I never saw him. He worked all the time. I don't consider what I do to be work, but I think I've inherited his workaholic determinism. I don't think until I was in my twenties did my dad ever speak to me about being in the Vietnam

War. Then he started telling me about people that he'd killed and things that he was involved in with Agent Orange."

He says, "My father and I both have some sort of heart disorder, a heart murmur. I was really sick when I was a kid. I had pneumonia four or five times and was always in the hospital, always underweight, scrawny, primed for a beating."

Phones ring in the other offices. Four lanes of traffic go by outside.

"When I was writing the book [his autobiography]," Manson says, "I hadn't really gotten to the conclusion of how similar I was to my grandfather. Until I got to the end of the book, that hadn't dawned on me. That as a kid, I'm looking at him as a monster because he's got women's clothing and dildos and all these things, and by the end of my story I've become far worse than my grandfather ever was.

"I don't think I've told anyone this," Manson says, "but what I found out over the last year is that my father and my grandfather never got along. My father came back from the Vietnam War and was kind of tossed out on the street and told he had to pay rent. There's something really dark about that I never liked. And my father told me last year that he'd found out that that's not his real father. Which was the strangest thing I'd ever heard, because it started to make sense that maybe he was treated poorly and had this weird relationship. It's really weird to think that he wasn't really my grandfather."

He says, "I suspect that there's so much death imagery because as a kid being afraid of death—because I was always sick and always had sick relatives—there was always a fear of death for a long time. There was a fear of the Devil. A fear of the end of the world. The Rapture—which is a Christian myth that I discovered doesn't even exist in the Bible. All of that I just ended up becoming. I ended up becoming what I was afraid of. That was my way of dealing with it."

In the attic, Manson deals his fifth card: the Hanged Man

"The fifth card is more of your recent past," he says. "It also is meant to mean some sort of change has taken place, in this case it could mean the fact that I've become extremely more focused and maybe in some ways have neglected friendships and relationships."

He says, "I was born in '69, and that year's become such a focus for a lot of things, especially this record, *Holy Wood*. Because '69 was the end of so many things. Everything in culture just changed so much, and I think it was real important that I was born then, too. Just the end of the sixties. The fact that Huxley and Kennedy died on the same day. To me, that opened up some kind of schism or gateway to what was going to happen. It all started to show parallels for me. Altamonte was like Woodstock '99. The house I live in, the Stones lived there when they wrote 'Let It Bleed.' I found *Cocksucker Blues*, an obscure film that they made, and it shows them in my living room writing 'Gimme Shelter.' And 'Gimme Shelter' was the song that was emblematic of the whole Altamonte tragedy. And then the Manson murders were something I've always obsessed over, since I was a child. That to me had the same media coverage as Columbine.

"The thing that always bothered me was," he says, "this is the exact same thing. Nixon came out and said Manson was guilty during the trial, because Nixon was being blamed for everything that was wrong about the culture. Then the same thing happened with Clinton saying, 'Why are these kids acting so violent? It must be Marilyn Manson. It must be this movie. It must be this game.' Then he turns the cheek and sends some bombs overseas to kill a bunch of people. And he's wondering why kids have bombs and they're killing people . . ."

Manson brings out watercolor paintings he's done, bright and dark colorful Rorshsach-test portraits of McGowen. Paintings he does with—not so much the paints as the murky rinse water he uses to clean his brushes. One shows the grinning heads of Eric Harris and Dylan Klebold impaled on the raised fingers of a peace sign.

"It turns out that they weren't fans," he says. "One Denver reporter did enough research to prove they disliked me because I was too commercial. They were into more underground stuff. It pissed me off that the media took one thing, and it just kept snowballing. And it was because I'm an easy target. I look guilty. And I was on tour at the time."

He says, "People always ask me, 'What would you have said to them if you could talk to them?' and my answer is, 'Nothing. I would've listened.' That's the problem. Nobody listened to what they were saying. If you'd listened, you'd have known what was going on."

He says, "Strangely, although music is something to listen to, I think music listens back because there's no judgments. A kid can find something he identifies with. Or an adult. Here's a place you can go to where there's no judgments. There's not someone telling you what to believe in."

Manson deals his sixth card: the Star

"This card is the future," he says. "The Star. This means great success."

He says, "For a long time, I never saw myself getting to this point. I never looked beyond this because I thought I was either going to destroy myself or someone was going to kill me in the process. So in some ways I have beaten the dream. And it is scary. It is like starting over, but that's good because that's what I needed. There's been a lot of little rebirths along the way, but now I feel like I've born over into where I started out, but with a different interpretation. I've gone back in time in a way, but now I have more ammunition, more knowledge to face the world."

He says, "The natural thing for me to do is to be involved in movies, but it really has to be on my terms. I think I feel more suited as a director than an actor, although I like to act. I'm talking to Jodorowsky, the guy who did *El Topo* and *The Holy Mountain.* He's a Spanish director who worked with Dalí. He wrote a script called *Able Cain* and it's a fantastic thing. He's had it for about fifteen years, and he hasn't wanted to do it, but he contacted me because I was the only person he wanted to work with. And the character is very different from what people know of me, and that's the only reason I'm interested because most people who approach me, they want me to do different versions of myself. It's not really a challenge of any sort."

In the spring of 2001, Manson plans to publish his first novel, called *Holy Wood*, a narrative that will cover his first three records. In the attic, he sits on the floor, leaning into the blue light from his laptop and reads the first chapter out loud, a magical, surreal, poetic story, crammed with detail and cut loose from traditional boring fiction. Fascinating, but for now, top secret.

He deals his seventh card: the High Priestess

"This one," he says, "I'm not sure about."

People who come to interview Manson, his publicist asks that they not publish the fact that he stands whenever a woman enters or leaves the room. After his father was disabled with a back injury, Manson bought his parents a home in California and supports them. When checking into hotels, he uses the name "Patrick Bateman," the serial-killing character from Bret Ellis's novel *American Psycho*.

He deals his eighth card: the World

"The World," he says, "placed appropriately here represents the environmental or outside things that can prevent you."

He says, "I had a great, interesting experience in Dublin. Because it's very Catholic, I did this performance on the European tour. I had this cross made of TVs that burst into flames, and I came out—I basically was just nude except for leather underwear. I'd painted myself all charred. I came onstage, the cross was on fire, and I saw people in the front row turn around and face the other direction. It was unbelievable. It was the greatest compliment in a performance. They were so offended—and it's unbelievable to me that someone could be that offended—that they turned around and looked the other way. Hundreds of people."

Manson deals his ninth card: the Tower

"The Tower is a very bad card," he says. "It means destruction, but in the way that this is read, it comes across like I'm going to have to go against pretty much everyone. In a revolutionary way, and there's going to be some sort of destruction. The fact that the end result is the sun means it probably won't be me. It will probably be the people who try to get in my way."

About his novel, he says, "The whole story if you take it from the beginning is parallel to my own but just told in metaphors and different symbols that I thought other people could draw from. It's about being innocent and naive, much like Adam was in Paradise before the fall from grace. And seeing something like 'Holy Wood,' which I used as a metaphor to represent what people think is the perfect world, the ideal that we're all supposed to live up to, the way we're supposed to look and act, and it's about wanting—your whole life—to fit into this world that doesn't think you belong, that doesn't like you, that beats you down every step of the way, fighting and fighting and fighting and finally getting there and realizing that now that you're there, everyone around you are the same people who kept you down in the first place. So you automatically hate everyone around you. You resent them for making you become part of this game you didn't realize you were buying into. You trade one prison cell for another in some ways.

"That becomes the revolution," he says, "to be idealistic enough that you think you can change the world, and what you find is you can't change anything but yourself."

McGowen calls from the airport, and promises to call again when her plane lands. In a week Manson will leave for Japan. In a month, he'll start a world tour in Minneapolis. Next spring his novel will complete the past decade of his life. After that, he'll start again.

"In some ways it feels like—not a burden, but a weight has been lifted by putting to rest a long-term project," he says. "It gives me the freedom to go anywhere. I feel a lot like I did ten years ago when I started the band. I feel that same drive and inspiration, and that same disdain for the world that makes me want to do something that makes people think.

"The only fear I have left is the fear of not being able to create, of not having inspiration," Manson says.

"I may fail, and this may not work but at least I'm choosing to do it. It's not something I'm doing because I'm stuck with it."

Manson deals his tenth card: the Sun

The two Boston terriers are curled up, asleep on a black velvet chair.

He says, "This is the final outcome, the Sun, which represents happiness and accomplishing a great deal."

{Bodhisattvas}

"We flew down through Miami to Tegucigalpa," Michelle Keating says, "and this was after five days of terror. There's land mines. There's snakes. There's starving people. The mayor of Tegucigalpa was killed the week before in a helicopter accident."

Looking at pictures in a pile of photo albums, Keating says, "This was Hurricane Mitch. I'd never imagined I would go to a disaster like that."

In October 1998, Hurricane Mitch struck the Republic of Honduras with 180 mph winds and days of heavy rain—twenty-five inches in a single day. Mountains collapsed. Rivers flooded. Some 9,071 people died in Central America, 5,657 in Honduras alone, where 8,058 people are still missing. One-point-four million were left homeless, and 70 percent of the country's crops were destroyed.

In the days after the storm, the capital city of Tegucigalpa was an open sewer, buried in mud and bodies. Malaria broke out. So did dengue fever. Rats carried leptospirosis, which causes liver and kidney failure and death. In this mining city, five thousand feet above sea level, one-third of all buildings were destroyed. The city's mayor died while surveying the damage in a helicopter. Looting was widespread.

In this country where 50 percent of the 6.5 million people live below the United Nations poverty level and 30 percent are unemployed, Michelle Keating and her golden retriever, Yogi, came to help find the dead.

She looks at a photo of Yogi sitting in an American Airlines seat, eating an airline meal off the tray in front of him.

Talking about another search-and-rescue volunteer, she says, "Harry said, 'These people are hungry and they might want to eat your dog.' And I was driving home from a meeting with him, I was going, 'I don't want to die!'—but I knew I wanted to go."

She looks at pictures of the fire station in Honduras where they slept. Rescue dogs from Mexico had already arrived but weren't much help. A dam above the city had collapsed at two in the morning.

"A forty-foot wall of water had gone through and then re-ceded, leaving just this deep, deep mud," Keating says. "Every-where the water and mud had touched a dead body, there was the smell. That's what was confusing the Mexican dogs. They were hitting everywhere."

Looking at photos of the swollen, muddy Choluteca River, she says, "There was dengue fever. There was the germs. Every-where you went, you could smell dead bodies there. And Yogi couldn't get away from it, and he wasn't wagging anymore at all. They had a water shortage, but we'd wash everything down as much as we could."

In the pictures, people shovel the mud out of the streets in exchange for government food. The smell of the dead was "pungent," she says. "You could taste it."

She says, "Ten thousand were killed throughout the whole country, and a good percentage of them were right there in Tegucigalpa, because they had the landslides, too. So there were the people drowned by the forty-foot wall of water coming through town. Then the soccer field caved in."

She shows photos of dim rooms, half-filled with dirt and broken furniture. She says, "The first day, we went to a Chinese restaurant where this family had died. The fire department would have to excavate, and what we were able to do is save a lot of time for them, and grief, because we'd pinpoint exactly where. In the Chinese restaurant we put Mentholatum under our noses and wore masks and a helmet with a light because it was dark. All the food, like crab, was spoiling and the sewers had overflowed, and it was knee-deep in mud. And there were all these dirty diapers. So Yogi and I go back into the kitchen, and I thought, 'Oh my gosh, what am I going to find?'"

In the photos, she's wearing a miner's hat with a light mounted on front, and a surgical mask of gauze.

"There was all their clothes and personal effects embedded in the mud," she says. "People's entire lives."

They found the dead, crushed and twisted. "It turned out they were under a platform. There was a low platform that tables and chairs were on, and the water had forced them under there."

Michelle's sitting on the sofa in her living room, the photo albums on a table in front of her. Yogi sits on the floor at her side. Another golden retriever, Maggie, sits in a club chair across the room. Both dogs are five and a half years old. Maggie came from an animal shelter after they found her, sick and starving, apparently abandoned by a breeder after she'd produced so many litters she couldn't have more.

Yogi she bought from a breeder when he was six months old and couldn't walk.

"It turned out that he has elbow dysplasia," she says, "and a couple years ago I took him to a vet in Eugene who did surgery to allow him to walk. It reseated the joint. What had been happening was, this small joint—it was supposed to be a strut, but it was taking the weight, so it was fragmenting, and it was very painful for him."

Looking at the dog in the club chair, she says, "Maggie's more the red, smaller kind. She's probably about seventy-five pounds. Yogi's the larger, blond, long-haired fellow. In the winter he's over ninety pounds. He's got the typical golden big butt."

Looking at older pictures, she says, "About eight years ago I had a dog named Murphy. He was border collie/Australian shepherd mix, an incredible dog, and I thought, 'Here's a good way to work obedience with him and maybe meet some people. I was working at Hewlett-Packard, in an office situation, so I needed a balance."

She says, "The more I did it, the more intrigued I was by the cases. It started out as this dog-focused obedience thing and evolved into something that *I* really had more of a passion for."

In the photos of Honduras, Michelle and Yogi work with fellow volunteer Harry Oakes, Jr., and his dog, Valorie, a mix of border collie, schipperke, and kelpie. Oakes and Valorie helped search the ruins of the Federal Courthouse after the Oklahoma City bombing.

"Valorie, when she smells a dead body—or what she's looking for—she'll start barking," says Michelle. "She's very vocal. Yogi, he'll wag and get very excited, but he barely says a word. If it's a deceased victim, he'll whine. His tail will go down and do the stress reaction."

She says, "Valorie will get hysterical and start crying. And she'll dig, if it's mud with someone underneath. Or if it's water, she'll jump in the water."

Looking at the photos of collapsed houses, she says, "When someone is either stressed or angry or anything, they let off epinephrine. And when violence or death happens, it's just a more intense release of those smells. Plus whatever gases and fluids belonged to the body when it died. You can imagine in the wild why that would be so important to a pack. To an animal that means, 'Something has been killed here. One of my pack members has been killed here.' They get particularly upset over a human, because we're part of their pack."

She says, "About ninety percent of the training to do search and rescue is the human recognizing what the dog's doing naturally. Being able to read Yogi when he's stressed.

"Obedience sets the tone that you're in charge," she says. "Then you hide toys from them; I still do that. And they love it. They have a race to see who can find it first. The next thing you do is have someone hold the dog while you run away and hide. You just keep doing more and more complex situations. They're looking on a track. If they haven't seen where you're going, they can smell."

Looking at a photo of a group of men, she says, "This is the Venezuelan fire brigade. We said we were the Pan-American rescue team."

About another photo, she says, "This is the one area we called the 'car graveyard.'"

About a vast, sliding hillside of mud, she says, "This is the soccer field that collapsed."

In another photo, inside a house filled with mud, she says, "Walking through this house that had been looted, there were handprints on the wall. All these mud prints where the looters had kept their balance."

In a wide band along all the walls are countless perfect handprints in brown mud.

In other photos are the rooms where Yogi found bodies buried under fallen walls, under mattresses.

One photo shows a neighborhood of houses tumbling down a steep cliff of mud.

"This is up on the hill where all these houses had collapsed," she says. "They had hundreds of stories why people wouldn't leave: they didn't want looters to get their stuff, a woman with kids said her husband had gone to a bar and told her to stay here. Just awful, tragic stories."

Another photo shows Valorie sleeping in the back of a pickup truck, dwarfed by a thick roll of dark plastic bags.

Michelle says, "That's Valorie with the body bags, exhausted."

She talks about her first search, saying, "It was up in Kelso, and it was a fellow whose wife had disappeared. There was word that she was fooling around with all types of different people who were coming up to the house. So we drive up to this immaculately manicured farm. There's horses and a pasture with a bull in it. The dogs did a huge death alert in the barn. Their tail goes down and they pee. They swallow a lot. The natural part is the defecating, that and the peeing and the whining and the crying. It's making them nauseated, I think. Yogi pulls away. He doesn't want to go near it. Valorie goes toward it and she digs and barks more and more, and she gets frantic because she's trying to communicate something. 'It's right here!'

"These people's little boy, he was about four, said something to the grandmother about 'Daddy put mommy underwater,' and they whisked him away and nobody was able to be alone with him after that."

In another picture from Tegucigalpa, a long slab of concrete lies on its side in the middle of a riverbed.

"That was a bridge," Michelle says.

In all the pictures are scattered little packages of rancid lard, left everywhere by the water.

"The most profound search that I'll still get choked up about was this autistic child," she says. "The little guy was four years old, and they'd locked him in, but he'd found a way to unlock the door while his mom was ironing upstairs. He'd take all his clothes off, too, as soon as he got out the door. So all these people had volunteered to go look. And that's not optimal, because every time one more person walks across the trail, they can track the scent somewhere else."

In these older photographs, Michelle is working with Rusty, another golden retriever. The photos show a heavy woods around a slow, dark slough of stagnant water.

"Within an hour of getting there, we got down to the slough. This is the primary spot because the little boy, he liked throwing a toy in repeatedly, and pulling it out. It was just a little bank above the slough with roots and trees around it."

She says, "By then Rust was real distraught and really sad. That was the first place where the kid went in, so there was a certain kind of scent there that wasn't as strong as when we followed the real slight current in the slough down to where it was getting stronger and stronger. That's when we called the divers in. There was a culvert between two parts of the slough."

Looking at the photos, she says, "What happened was the body had gotten wedged in this culvert, and it was under mud."

Petting Yogi, she says, "This is quite a large water area, and I'm going around, getting death alerts all around this huge marsh area. And I'm marking everywhere we get the hits. All that water that had touched the body had the smell of the death on it. Sometimes you can triangulate and determine where the body is by where the alerts are coming from.

"Putting a tag, and where the wind was coming from," she says. "What the temperature was. Who I was. What time it was. We put it all on a map. To figure out where the body had drifted to.

"Air scenting . . . In a case where you don't know exactly where the person started, there's still the scent in the air. There's a scent cone that goes like this"—she waves hands in the air—"and you can get the dog to work a Z pattern. They might do it naturally. You want them to go toward the source of the scent."

Still petting Yogi, Michelle blinks, her eyes bright with tears. She says, "I look up, and they're pulling him out of the culvert. That's the only victim I've ever seen, because most of the time, like in Honduras, they come in and dig the victims out after we've left. But I went into deep shock the moment I saw him, and I had this profound urge to just hold him, this little guy."

She says, "We got up to the house and did different interviews and then went into the house to cheer up the family—because the dogs are supposed to cheer up the family—and it was like walking through this aura, this energy—like an environmental condition . . . like being in a fog.

"We didn't process this like we should have," Michelle says. "I came back home and put Rusty with the other two dogs, to play, and I went off to work. I've always felt like that stuck with him too long because I didn't debrief him, and I don't think I knew how to process it. I don't think I understood what happened—as far as the deep shock—until I went to Honduras.

"You're supposed to let them go find a live person—and I did do that. You make sure, too, that you wash everything. Their jacket. My clothes. Everything that they have on. Wash everything in the car, everything that could've come in contact with the death scent. Just a little bit of that scent and they're depressed again."

She says, "Going back home, the scent pretty much permeated the car, so it would've been good to clean that out as well."

Rusty and Murphy, Michelle's border collie/shepherd mix—like all the victims they found—are dead now. Murphy was put down when he was fourteen and a half years old, after suffering with back problem for three years. Rusty was put down after his kidneys failed.

Looking at photos of children, children hugging Yogi in picture after picture, Michelle talks about meeting a little girl in Tegucigalpa. Her legs running with staph infections, the girl was dipping water out of a puddle of sewage. Michelle put disinfecting tablets in the girl's water. A journalist rubbed antibiotic cream on the girl's legs.

"We had to walk most places because there was the mud, and everyone who saw Yogi would smile," she says. "And if we stopped somewhere, they'd just swarm around to touch him and say, '*Dame lo! Dame lo!* Give him to me!' And he was just thrilled with it. He loved the attention. I know he understood how important the work was, and I'd tried to explain to him along the way, 'This is very important. You're doing good things for people.'"

In a picture of the collapsed soccer field, Michelle points out a crowd that stands at the far edge. "People would stand up here on the edge of the field and just watch us, and this one little boy said, 'Thank you,' in English."

She says, "Stuff like that would just destroy me. It was just too heartbreaking to have human contact like that."

She smiles over one picture, saying, "We went to an orphanage to cheer up the dogs. A kid would run and hide, and then the dogs would find him."

Over the next picture, she says, "This is an island. We drove two hours over washboard roads and hairpin turns in the back of a dump truck to get there. This is the back of the dump truck, it's real dusty. We found three bodies."

She pets Yogi, saying, "I think it aged him. He's seen and smelled things most two-year-old pups won't have to go through."

In another photo album, Yogi sits with very thin, smiling men.

"I believe in Bodhisattvas," Michelle says. "In Buddhism, there are beings that are enlightened, and they come back to help others. I think Yogi's purpose in being with me is to help me be a better person and do things. For me, walking into Our House would've been difficult without him, but with him it was like home."

Talking about the AIDS hospice where she now takes Yogi, Michelle says, "I wanted something that was compelling and meaningful, and I kept hearing about Our House from people. At first I asked if they wanted someone to do Reiki, and they said no. Then I said I had this really neat dog, and they said come on over. And that was it. We just started going there every week."

"A lot of them have just lost a pet," she says. "Sometimes that's the mitigating factor: *Well, if I have a pet I can't move into Our House.* And then the pet dies, and there is a lot of grief associated with that. And anyone who lives there is a little like a refugee. They've lost at least a lover. And, materially, they've lost their household."

Scratching Yogi's ears, Michelle says, "That's just part of his job. The comforting. That's what I mean by the Bodhisattva, that he's more concerned with comforting and helping, almost even more than his own well-being."

She says, "The trip to Honduras was a real seminal moment for me. One of those watershed moments. It was a high in a certain way. You never wondered what your purpose was while you were there because it was so clear. You could just be totally immersed in it."

Both dogs are asleep now on club chairs in this gray ranch house in the suburbs. The backyard is outside sliding glass patio doors, pocked with mud from the dogs running around.

"Prior to going to Honduras, I'd just finished school," Michelle says. "I'd just got my master's, and I'd left Hewlett-Packard. It was like, 'Hey, there's this whole multidimensional world out there beyond trying to fit in stupid corporate culture. Where's the meaning *there?*' One day of searching in Honduras—and I consciously thought this while I was down there—is exponentially more meaningful than twenty years in the corporate world.

"It's just so beautiful," Michelle says. "Part of me cries, still, when I see a dog working, whether it be a Seeing Eye dog or a Yogi when he's at his best. I'm just in awe of it."

She closes the album of Tegucigalpa, Honduras—the pictures of Hurricane Mitch—and puts the album on a stack of albums.

She says, "It was just eight days. I think we did what we could."

{Human Error}

You've probably seen Brian Walker on television. If not, you heard him on the radio. You saw him chatting with Conan O'Brien, or on *Good Morning America*. Or he was on with Howard Stern one morning.

He's the guy. That guy. You know, the first person to build his own rocket—yes, right there in his backyard in Bend, Oregon—and shoot himself into outer space.

He calls himself "Rocket Guy."

Yes, of course. *That* guy.

Now you remember. In the hundreds of radio and television spots, in the newspaper and magazine articles, you're heard the logistics. How his rocket is fiberglass, powered by a 90 percent solution of hydrogen peroxide exposed to a screen plated with silver.

"It's like when you mix vinegar and baking soda," Rocket Guy would tell you. "It's a chemical reaction. The peroxide hits the silver and it causes a catalytic conversion that changes it into steam. And the steam then expands. Basically, the peroxide turns to superheated steam of about thirteen hundred degrees and expands six hundred times in volume."

A blast of compressed air will assist the rocket's launch. It will go fifty miles straight up, then fall down, slowed by a parasail.

He's the rich toy inventor. Engaged to marry the beautiful Russian woman he met on the Internet and dated while training with Russian cosmonauts.

Yes, of course you've heard of him and his "Project R.U.S.H." Meaning: *Rapid Up Super High*. The guy with just a high school education. You probably heard him on Art Bell's radio show and then sent him an email. If you did, then you got an answer. Rocket Guy has answered thousands of your emails. Asking for advice about your inventions. Telling him how much your kid loves his toys. And, what's amazing is, he answered you. Maybe even sent you a toy.

He's your hero. Or you think he's a big-mouth fraud.

Yeah, *that guy* . . . What ever happened to him?

Oh, he's still there. Well, he is and he isn't.

If you sent him an email—at www.rocketguy.com—chances are it's still on his computer. If you sent him an email, you're a little part of the problem.

In December 2001, Rocket Guy was working in his shop, working on the hydraulic lift part of the trailer that would haul his rocket to the launch site. It's thirty degrees outside, and the high desert is ankle-deep with snow. The twelve acres where

Brian Walker lives, a one-song drive from the center of town, is mostly pine trees and lava rock. He lives in a big log cabin. A short walk downhill are his garage and his shop buildings. Beside them is his "Rocket Garden," an array of equipment he built to train for his trip into the atmosphere.

Sticking out of the snow, you'll see bright red and yellow, foam and fiberglass prototypes for missiles and capsules and rockets. In his shop, the white walls are hung with the prototypes for toys he's invented. Brian Walker is big and bearded, and his part-time helper, Dave Engeman, is small and clean-shaven, and, with the snow and the toys, the pine trees and the log cabin, the two men suggest a workshop somewhere near the North Pole. More like elves than astronauts.

If you ask, Rocket Guy will take toys down off the wall and demonstrate the ones that he could never sell. "It's tough, trying to make toys these days," he says. "The Consumer Product Safety Administration is so anal about how something could be misused. In the good old days, you could buy toys that, if you misused them, you could lose an eye or a finger."

Here's a tented stretcher he designed for the army. Here's a go-cart the size of a suitcase. Showing you the failures, hundreds of plastic and wood prototypes stored in crates, he says, "I want to do a line of toys called 'The Better Tomorrow Toys.' They're going to be designed so that if a child had an IQ below a certain level, they wouldn't survive the toy. So you weed out the gene pool at a young age. Stupid kids are not nearly as dangerous as stupid adults, so let's take them out when they're young. I know it sounds cruel, but it's a reasonable expectation."

He laughs and says, "Of course that's all a joke. Just like the line of toys I want to do for blind kids, called 'Out of Sight Toys' . . ."

At the rear end of the rocket trailer, he's mounting a steel tank. It sits below four tall pipes that will slip up, inside the rocket. At takeoff, high-pressure air from the tank, channeled through the four pipes, will give the rocket its initial lift.

"The blast of air gives it momentum," Brian says. "If I have a twelve-thousand-pound thrust motor and a rocket that weighs a thousand pounds with nine thousand pounds of fuel, then I have a takeoff weight of ten thousand pounds, and twelve thousand pounds of thrust. If the air launch gives me a boost, then I have zero weight, so the twelve thousand pounds of thrust is immediately applied to thrust so I leave the ground with a more positive attitude and a much more stable launch."

In a nutshell, that's rocket science. At least for the first test flight. Inside the rocket there's no controls so there's no chance of human error. Simple as that.

"I'm not a rocket scientist," Brian says. "Everything I'm doing is public knowledge. I'm using information gleaned from fifty years of the space program. My rocket is more or less a giant toy. It's a big toy on steroids."

He says, "The moment I open the valve to the engine, that's when you launch the air. I want the engine at full throttle before I release the air pressure. If for some reason the engine didn't fire at the moment I launched, I'd get about fifty feet up and then come back down. The parachute wouldn't help, and the weight would be so much I couldn't even separate the capsule from the fuel tank. The moment the engine throttle is opened, the compressed air goes."

Hydrogen peroxide turning to steam . . . A push of air—just like Brian's toy Pop-It Rocket, which you can buy at Target and Disneyland . . . And Brian himself standing upright in the nose of the thirty-foot-long rocket.

"When it launches—boom—I'm up," he says. "And when I

get to apogee, the highest point, the nose cone pops off and a parachute comes out. Then, as I'm descending, two doors snap open and there's going to be a little catapult seat that just rolls me right out. And I skydive."

It's that simple.

He'll be traveling at mach 4 when the main engine runs out of fuel. His capsule will separate from the fuel tank and coast for four and one-half minutes, until he reaches peak height, at about six minutes after launch.

"The acceleration phase is ninety seconds," he says, "and the whole flight should last about fifteen minutes from launch to when I touch down."

Fins made of compression-molded Styrofoam will help stabilize the rocket, then drop off in two stages, getting smaller and smaller as the rocket gains speed. His first manned test rocket will travel fifteen thousand feet, almost three miles, straight up. Then straight down, more or less.

"It's not like I'm going to have a lot of stuff falling," he says. "I'm going to have eight fin sections, fluttering down like leaves. And that one fuel tank. And I plan to have the fuel tank recovered for posterity, because I plan on having my capsule and the fuel tank and the whole rocket hanging in the Smithsonian Museum or some other prominent air and space museum. I talked to the Smithsonian and they said, yeah, if I build and launch my own private rocket, and it's the first one, they definitely will hang it."

That's the plan, fifteen minutes of fame and then straight into the history books.

All this will take place in Nevada's Black Rock Desert—where the annual Burning Man festival is held—the only place that can accommodate the quarter of a million people Brian expects to attend.

This has been Brian Walker's dream since he was nine years old. His father took him to his first air show when Brian was twelve. Two weeks after he turned sixteen, he made his first skydive. In 1974, when he was eighteen years old, he was almost dragged behind the plane while making a static-line jump. He froze, his hands locked on the wing, and the plane had to land with him still hanging there. He didn't jump again for seventeen years.

About his education, Brian will tell you, "I'm dyslexic, and ADHD, and school was torture for me. I tried two terms in college, to take engineering, and it was more or less to appease my dad. I took two terms toward a mechanical engineering degree at OIT and decided, 'This is not what I want.' The partying almost killed me. The only thing I could do to maintain my sanity was to stay as mind-altered as possible."

He tends to get plantar warts, and uses a plasma welder to burn them off. "It's great for removing warts," he says. "But it leaves a nice little crater in your foot. As quick as I can pull and release the trigger, it sends a pulse of plasma that vaporizes the skin. It hurts like *hell*."

He says, "I used a soldering iron once before."

For Brian, five hours is a good night's sleep. Despite new pillows and a down comforter, he's an insomniac, just like his dad. He has no hobbies, other than inventing. He doesn't use the Lord's name in vain and says a Britney Spears concert is just a sex show. And doesn't approve of the Harry Potter books, because of the witchcraft. He has no pet, not right now in 2001, but he had a flying squirrel named Benny that died of an aneurysm after nine years. After that, he had a sugar glider, explaining, "It's the marsupial equivalent of a flying squirrel." For the movie version of his life, he'd cast Mel Gibson or Heath Ledger.

"Growing up," he says, "I was just never a big sports person. I just had a feeling that I was viewed as being less of a man since I didn't know statistics about players of sports. I just have this really jaded view that sports has become artificially elevated to a level of importance that it shouldn't have. They seem to want to make an art and an entire lifestyle out of analyzing games and players. You go into every single bar in America and all they show on the TV is sports and sports shows. And I have to be honest, in every basketball game I've ever watched—and I've watched quite a few—I've never seen anything new. I'm just a little bit bothered by the fact that, if you're not an ardent, hardened sports fan who knows all the aspects of the game, then somehow you're not really a *man's* man."

In a sports bar, at lunch, he stops talking to watch a computer graphic on television showing an electromagnetic pulse "E bomb" explode over a city. He orders a Big Bad Bob Burger with an extra slice of raw onion. Even in December, he drinks ice water. He grew up in the Parkrose district of Portland, Oregon.

Over lunch, he complains about how American astronauts get a lifetime of training and experience at taxpayer expense and then make their fortune as celebrities based on that experience. Then, how wealthy American citizens have been slammed in the public mind for paying money to ride along on Russian space missions. How the dream of space travel needs to be opened up to people who don't want a lifelong military career.

He'd like to replace the income tax with a national sales tax.

At this point, in 2001, Brian's forty-five years old and engaged to marry a woman named Ilena (not her real name, for reasons you'll understand later), a Russian he met through a website called "A Foreign Affair."

This is the Rocket Guy you've already met. He likes cinnamon Altoids better than regular ones. He's flown in Russian

MIG fighters and choked back puke while experiencing zero-gravity dives aboard the "Vomit Comet" plane used to train cosmonauts. He's never been married, but he's ready now.

"My goal," he'll tell you, "is to find a woman who will enjoy life without the necessity of feeling like she has to go out and prove something. That, unfortunately, is what so many women in this culture feel they need to do. The feminist movement in the late sixties and early seventies convinced women that motherhood and being a stay-at-home mom was a lonely existence and not important. Unless you had a career you weren't anything."

Over his hamburger, he says, "One of my missions in life is to do the most I can to foster U.S. and Russian relations. The Cold War's over. Get over it. These people are not our enemy. The Russians are people who want to be just like us. They really love America and love us and what we stand for. And they want to be just like us. I think having a Russian wife will make it inevitable that I find myself speaking in this role."

After lunch he checks his mailbox, and there's a check for $55.06 from a Scottish radio interview. The only money he says he's made from the landslide of Rocket Guy publicity.

This is the Brian Walker the media discovered in April 2000.

"I wanted to be called *something*," he remembers, "but I didn't want to be called 'Rocket Man.' It was too formal-sounding. And too overused. 'Rocket Guy' has a whole lot more *friendly* sound to it. He's just like the guy next door. The man on the street. The name Rocket Guy just kind of stuck."

Beginning with one interview for a Florida newspaper, Rocket Guy was born, an international media celebrity doing two or three interviews each day. Getting so many phone calls his message system maxed out after the first hundred. His website had as many as 380,000 hits in one hour.

"Out of all the radio interviews I've done, there's only been two or three, maybe a dozen, where the radio personalities were trying to make me look like a fool," he says. "Even when I did Howard Stern, for a half-hour, he did not make fun of me. He did not make me out to be a kook. He made a couple references about 'am I getting laid more often now,' but he didn't turn it into a giant penis, sex thing, phallic symbol."

Still, what goes up, must come down.

And even Rocket Guy would tell you: reentry can be a bitch.

Brian and Ilena met in person for the first time in April 2001. Two months later, they spent another two weeks together and became engaged. In July of 2002, Ilena and her eight-year-old son, Alexi, arrived in America on a fiancée visa.

"I didn't want to believe I could make that big a mistake," Brian says. "We had eleven-hundred fifty-five emails between us over a year-and-a-half period. I wanted to believe her so much that I was willing to take the chance, but as soon as we got married, on October 15, 2002, then things just got worse."

Ilena was fifteen years younger than Brian, leaving behind a 700-square-foot apartment she'd shared with seven other people in Russia. Brian had installed a swimming pool for her son. He'd agreed to pay for her $4,000 in laser eye surgery and $12,000 in dental work. He'd traded in his BMW roadster for a sedan. Still, they fought. She refused to speak English at dinner, or to get out of bed before eight in the morning.

Brian brought home a computer for her to use while Alexi was at school all day. Six weeks later, he asked her about the Web surfing she'd done . . .

"The worst websites were for bestiality and sex with animals," he says. "She had been spending an hour or an hour and a half at a time, several days a week, going to these sites. It was only six weeks between when we got the computer and when she left. I was severely despondent to think this woman who I had loved enough to bring from Russia and marry was that perverse. We're not talking about normal porno, I'm talking about stuff that would make you *sick*."

Six weeks into the marriage and she'd secretly placed online ads, looking for a new man, ideally an artsy type with long blond hair, living in a city loft—pretty much the polar opposite of brunet, bearded Brian in his log cabin.

"Ilena is a very beautiful woman, but she has no soul. She's soulless," he says. "I'm convinced I was nothing more than a ticket here. That's all."

In Brian Walker's mind, Project R.U.S.H. was connected with being Rocket Guy and being married to Ilena. "I was thinking—in my own little way—what a great way to bring the world together," he says. "To show cooperation and connection between former enemies. We used to talk about how the two of us could do a book together. We could write children's books in English and Russian. I could see a whole tree growing out of this with all these opportunities, and that was just squashed."

The first time he talked to her about her Web surfing, Ilena packed a bag, took her son, and moved in with a neighbor—a Russian man she's been living with ever since.

Brian says, "I've had a lot of guys email me, and their stories were almost identical. These guys believed there was love there, but once their wife had her residency or her green card, she was gone. Ilena didn't even wait that long. She left two months after we were married. She couldn't even play the game long enough to get legal status."

That's where everything fell apart. Brian didn't eat for eight weeks. He lost forty-five pounds, shaved his beard, and couldn't bear to work on the rocket.

"I've been working so hard for so long," he says. "You go back to before I started this rocket project and look at the fifteen years of abject failure. I built a submarine, but I never made it into a business. I'd succeed in one portion, but I'd fail at a different part. The same with my stretcher or my hundreds of other inventions. I would work nonstop for months and years on end. Then I started getting success in the toy industry, and instead of scaling back I jumped into this project, and at this point in time it's completely overwhelming me."

Another shock came in the form of the "X-Prize," an offer of ten million dollars prize money to the first private group to put a rocket into the atmosphere. And the sudden competition Rocket Guy now faces from well-funded and well-educated teams around the world.

Even the media attention had become a handicap. Some two thousand people have shown up at his door, wanting a tour. "I have a really hard time saying no to people," he says. "What's slowed me down the most over the past three years is my desire to appease people's requests. Whether it's the media. Whether it's reading and answering emails or inviting people out to see things. Or doing school fund-raisers. I go speak at schools quite a bit."

It's been quite a ride. Money. Fame. Love. All of it before the rocket even got to the launch pad.

Fast-forward to July 2003, and, day by day, Brian Walker is coming back. A friend introduced him to a woman, an American, a realtor his own age. Her name is Laura, and already her voice is on his answering-machine message. They've skydived, together. There's even talk about another wedding—after Brian's divorce is final.

And he still gets letters, hundreds of letters from kids, parents, and teachers who love his toys.

There in Bend, Oregon, work continues in the Rocket Garden. There's the centrifuge where Brian trains himself to endure G forces. There's the tower where he tests rocket engines. In a couple months he plans to launch himself three miles high in a test rocket. He plans to finish the geodesic dome he's started. And the observatory perched on top of it. Inside the dome, the rocket waits, painted two-toned, light and dark blue. Ready, on the trailer he was making back in December 2001. Back when anything seemed possible. Love. Fame. Family.

In a way, it's all still possible.

Instead of instruments inside the rocket, he only wants a flat-screen video monitor hooked up to cameras on the outside. Or video goggles he can wear.

He wants to build a rocket sled that will ramp up one side of the dome.

He wants to design a glider-type aircraft that can be catapulted from city to city.

There's a go-cart he's building, powered by twin jet engines.

And the jet engine he bought on eBay and rigged so its 1,600-degree exhaust will melt the ice in his driveway . . . "When this thing kicks to life, your nuts suck all the way up into your stomach," he says. "It's almost terrifying to see this thing come to life."

And there's corporate sponsorship to search for. "I'd love Viagra as a sponsor, because the rocket makes a damn good symbol for Viagra," Brian Walker says. "Much better than a race car."

There's so much work left to do.

He still needs to distill the nine thousand pounds of hydrogen peroxide. And answer the emails. In the log cabin, his Soviet-made space suit waits.

The whole world waits.

Yes, you'll be hearing a lot more from Rocket Guy.

A lot more.

If he's not the first private person into space, then he wants to pioneer high-altitude skydiving from rockets. He wants to launch space tourism, which will allow people to orbit the Earth in a station, like a cruise ship, and drop out of the sky to visit any place, like a port. He plans to write a book that explains his success as an inventor. He's designing a carbon-fiber cannon that will shoot three-hundred-gallon water balloons to put out forest fires five miles away.

Inside his forty-five-foot-wide geodesic dome, Brian Walker talks about the red, green, and yellow halogen lights he plans to install. He talks about his other dreams. Of being "Teleportation Guy" and instantly teleporting himself to Russia. Or being "Time Travel Guy."

For now, he says, "The only thing reasonable I think I can do is to shoot myself into space. I can't time-travel. I can't teleport myself."

Inside the cool, dark dome, away from the desert sunshine, alone here with his rocket, he says, "I want to have unique special-effects lighting, and I want to have speakers that will make reverberating sounds so I can do really cool presentations."

You see, the way Rocket Guy explains it, the goal—space travel, time travel, teleportation—isn't your real reward. It's what you discover along the way. The same way putting a man on the moon gave us Teflon frying pans.

"And," Brian Walker says, "I want to do my own kind of

Kentucky Fried Movie type of thing. Remember the TV show *Time Tunnel?*"

He says, "I want to do *Time Tunnel 2001* with 'Time Guy,' and Time Guy's whole mission is to go back in time to nail significant historical babes so he can spread his genetic genes into the future. So he goes back to Egypt to get with Cleopatra, and the moment he arrives he turns around and he's just about to be trampled by chariots, so they zap him back to the future. And then he goes back to France to get with Marie Antoinette, and he materializes on the guillotine just as the blade is coming down. So every time this poor sap goes back in time, he arrives at a point where within seconds he's going to be dead. And, the poor guy, it ends up he never does anything . . ."

{Dear Mr. Levin,}

In college, we had to read about people shown pictures of gum disease. These were photographs of rotten gums and crooked, stained teeth, and the idea was to see how these images would affect the way people cared for their own teeth.

One group was shown mouths only a little rotten. The second group was shown moderately rotten gums. The third group was shown horrible blackened mouths, the gums peeled down, soft and bleeding, the teeth turned brown or missing.

The first study group, they took care of their teeth the same as they always had. The second group, they brushed and flossed a little more. The third group, they just gave up. They stopped brushing and flossing and just waited for their teeth to turn black.

This effect the study called "narcotization."

When the problem looks too big, when we're shown too much reality, we tend to shut down. We become resigned. We fail to take any action because disaster seems so inevitable. We're trapped. This is narcotization.

In a culture where people get too scared to face gum disease, how do you get them to face anything? Pollution? Equal rights? And how do you prompt them to fight?

This is what you, Mr. Ira Levin, do so very well. In a word, you *charm* people.

Your books, they're not so much horror stories as cautionary fables. You write a smart, updated version of the kind of folksy legends that cultures have always used—like nursery rhymes and stained-glass windows—to teach some basic idea to people. Your books, including *Rosemary's Baby*, *The Stepford Wives*, and *Sliver*, take some of the thorniest issues in our culture and *charm* us into facing the problem. As recreation. You turn this kind of therapy into fun. On our lunch breaks, waiting for a bus, lying in bed, you have us face these Big Issues, and fighting them.

What's creepy is, these are issues the American public is years away from confronting, but in each one—in each book— you ready us for a battle you seem to see coming. And, so far, you're always right.

In *Rosemary's Baby*, published in 1967, the battle is over a woman's right to control her own body. The right to good health care. And the right to choose an abortion. She's controlled by her religion, by her husband, by her male best friend, by her male obstetrician.

All this you got people to read—to pay *money* to read—years before the feminist health-care movement. The Boston Women's Health Cooperative. *Our Bodies, Ourselves*. And consciousness-raising groups where women would sit around with a speculum and flashlight and look at changes in each other's cervix.

You showed women exactly how *not* to be. What *not* to do. Do *not* just sit around your apartment sewing cushions for the window seats and not asking questions. Take some responsibility. If you get date-raped by the Devil, don't think twice about terminating that pregnancy. And, yes, it's silly. The Devil . . . And the fact he has a big, BIG erection. And Rosemary is tied down, spread-eagled by Jackie Kennedy, aboard a yacht during a storm at sea. What would Carl Jung make of all that? Nevertheless, that's what lets us inside. We can pretend this is all a fantasy. It's not real, abortion isn't a real issue. We can feel Rosemary's joy, her terror and rage.

Did you anticipate that now, in a creepy echo thirty years later, backlash against abortion rights gives the fetus a legal right to be born in many states? In courtrooms, women have become "gestation hosts" or "gestation carriers," forced by legal action to carry and give birth to children they don't want. Fetuses have become symbols for antiabortion foes to rally around. The way Rosemary's neighbors rallied around her baby in its black-draped crib.

Another funny, creepy part is—our body doesn't know this isn't real. We're so wrapped up in this story, we get a cathartic experience. A horrible adventure by proxy. Like Rosemary, we're smarter now. We're not going to make this same mistake. Nope. No more bossy doctors. No more sleazy husbands. No more getting drunk and being knocked up by the Devil.

And just in case, let's make abortion an okay, legal option. Case closed.

Mr. Levin, your skill to tell an important, threatening story through a metaphor, maybe it comes from your experience writing for television's "golden age," shows like *Lights Out* and *The United States Steel Hour*. This was television in the 1950s and early '60s, when most issues had to be masked or disguised to avoid offending a conservative audience and the even more conservative sponsors of a program. In a time before "transgressive fiction," such as *The Monkey Wrench Gang*, *American Psycho*, and *Trainspotting*, where a writer could stand on a soap box and shout about a social issue, your writing career started in this era, in the most public form of writing, when the mask, the metaphor, the *disguise* was everything.

Good theater and social commentary had to mix well with commercials for soap and cigarettes.

What's important is, it worked. And it still works. The fable lifts an issue free from its specific time and makes it important to people for years to come. The metaphor even *becomes* the issue, injecting it with humor, and giving people a new freedom to laugh at what had scared them before. Your best example of this is *The Stepford Wives*.

Published in 1972, the book shows a woman with a family and an embryonic career as a professional photographer. She's just moved out of the city, into the countryside town of Stepford. There, all the wives seem devoted to nothing except serving their husbands and families. They're all physical, big-breasted, pretty ideals. They clean and cook. And, well, that's it. Reading the book, we follow Joanna Eberhart and her two friends as, one by one, they give up their personal ambitions and resign themselves to cooking and cleaning.

The creepy part is, the Stepford husbands are killing their wives. Working as a group, the men are replacing the women with lovely, efficient robots that do everything asked of them.

The *even creepier part* is, you wrote this more than a decade before the rest of American culture noticed the men's "back-lash" against women's liberation. It wasn't until the Pulitzer Prize–winning book *Backlash*, by Susan Faludi, that someone besides you acknowledged the idea that men might organize and fight to keep women in traditionally female roles.

And, yes, *Backlash* is an excellent book, and it makes its case by describing how male fashion designers dress women, and how antiabortion people dismiss women as just the vehicles for an unborn fetus, but the message there is so . . . strident. There's no charm here. Ms. Faludi points out a problem and piles on the evidence, but when the book is done, she leaves us with no feeling of resolution. No freedom. No personal trans-formation.

Worse—like in so much transgressive fiction, where the au-thor gets to blatantly rant about problems—narcotization sets in. The message gets so blatant and relentless that people stop hearing it.

But in *Stepford Wives*, wow, we laugh with Bobbie and Joanna. We laugh a lot, all through the first half of the book. Then Charmaine disappears. Then poor Bobbie. Then Joanna. The horror cycle is complete. We've seen what happens when you play dumb and deny reality until it's too late. Now, all those nice homemakers rolling pie crust in clean, sunny kitchens, we see them as tainted, as manipulated and shaped. As Stepford wives.

Your silly, crazy robot metaphor, it's so . . . over the top. Crazy as it looks, it's replaced all the tired dogmatic rant about housework as demeaning, blah, blah, blah. Your Disney-female-robot-sex-slave-hausfrau metaphor is even better than your big-dick-Devil-date-rape metaphor.

You leave us with just the clear message: housework = death.

A simple, memorable, modern fable. Do not let anyone make you into a Stepford wife. Develop your own career beyond being a wife.

In each book, you create a metaphor that allows us to face a Big Issue without being so confronted we give up hope and retreat. First, you charm us with humor, then you scare us with a worst-case scenario. You show us someone who gets trapped, who refuses to recognize and deal with the danger until it's too late.

You might not agree, but even in *Sliver*, published in 1991, the main character fails to wise up until it's too late.

Ten years before the rest of the world tuned into "reality television" and webcams hidden in tanning salons, locker rooms and public toilets, again you predict the battle over privacy in the face of new broadcast and video technology. In *Sliver*, Kay Norris moves into a lovely apartment on the twentieth floor of a narrow "sliver" building in Manhattan. She falls in love with a younger man, another resident of the building, not knowing he owns the building. And he's wired every apartment with hidden cameras that allow him to watch the residents as entertainment.

The darker secret of the "horror high-rise" is that as people discover their phones are bugged and their apartments are being spied on, the young building owner murders them. He even records the murders and keeps the tapes.

Like Rosemary Woodhouse and Joanna Eberhart, Kay thinks her apartment is a great new beginning. Despite fellow residents dying all around her, she clings to her denial and distracts herself with her love affair. In an interesting evolution from Rosemary (who had no career) through Joanna (who snapped a few pictures), Kay Norris is consumed by her job as a book editor. She's never been married. And she isn't destroyed by the reality she failed to recognize.

But only because her cat saves her—hardly her own doing.

Ten years before states realized they had no laws that forbid someone from carrying a camera in a suitcase, then standing in a crowd and filming up the bottom of women's skirts, a decade ago, you tried to warn us. This was possible. Technology had outdistanced law, and this was going to happen. Then you created a fable to get our attention and inoculate us against the fear by creating a metaphor, a character that models the wrong behavior.

Was it Plato who made his arguments by telling a story with an obvious flaw, and allowing the listener to realize the error? Whoever it was, that method gives the reader the moment of realization, the emotional moment of "ah-hah!" And teaching experts say that, unless we have that moment of chaos, followed by the emotional release of realization, nothing will be remembered. In this way you, Mr. Ira Levin, force us to remember the mistakes made by your characters.

Oh, Mr. Ira Levin, how do you do it? You show us the future. Then you help us deal with that scary new world. You take us, fast, straight through a worst-case scenario and let us live it.

In the therapy called "flooding," a psychologist will force a patient to endure an exaggerated scenario of his or her worst fear. To overload the emotions. A person afraid of spiders might be locked in a room filled with spiders. A person afraid of snakes might be forced to handle snakes. The idea is that contact and familiarity will dull the terror the patient has for something they've been too afraid to explore. The actual experience, the reality of what snakes feel like and how they act, it destroys the fear by contradicting the patient's expectation.

Is that it, Mr. Levin? Is that what you're up to?

Or is what you do just consolation? Showing us the worst so

our lives look better by comparison. No matter how controlling our doctor seems, at least *we're* not giving birth to a devil baby. No matter how boring the suburbs feel, at least *we're* not dead and replaced by a robot.

Your fellow writer Stephen King once said that horror novels give us a chance to rehearse our deaths. The horror writer is like a Welsh "sin eater," who absorbs the faults of a culture and diffuses them, leaving the reader with less fear of dying. You, Mr. Levin, are almost the opposite. In big, funny, scary ways, you acknowledge our faults. The problems we're too afraid to recognize.

And by writing, you give us less to fear about living.

That's very, VERY creepy, Mr. Levin. But not creepy-bad. It's creepy-*nice*. Creepy-*great*.

PERSONAL

{Escort}

My first day as an escort, my first "date" had only one leg. He'd
gone to a gay bathhouse, to get warm, he told me. Maybe for
sex. And he'd fallen asleep in the steam room, too close to the
heating element. He'd been unconscious for hours, until someone found him. Until the meat of his left thigh was completely
and thoroughly cooked.

He couldn't walk, but his mother was coming from Wisconsin to see him, and the hospice needed someone to cart the two
of them around to visit the local tourist sights. Go shopping
downtown. See the beach. Multnomah Falls. This was all you
could do as a volunteer if you weren't a nurse or a cook or
doctor.

You were an escort, and this was the place where young people with no insurance went to die. The hospice name, I don't even remember. It wasn't on any signs anywhere, and they asked you to be discreet coming and going because the neighbors didn't know what was going on in the enormous old house on their street, a street with its share of crack houses and drive-by shootings, still nobody wanted to live next door to this: four people dying in the living room, two in the dining room. At least two people lay dying in each upstairs bedroom, and there were a lot of bedrooms. At least half these people had AIDS, but the house didn't discriminate. You could come here and die of anything.

The reason I was there was my job. This meant lying on my back on a creeper with a two-hundred-pound class-8 diesel truck driveline lying on my chest and running down between my legs as far as my feet. My job is I had to roll under trucks as they crept down an assembly line, and I installed these drive-lines. Twenty-six drivelines every eight hours. Working fast as each truck moved along, pulling me into the huge blazing-hot paint ovens just a few feet down the line.

My degree in journalism couldn't get me more than five dollars an hour. Other guys in the shop had the same degree, and we joked how liberal arts degrees should include welding skills so you'd at least pick up the extra two bucks an hour our shop paid grunts who could weld. Someone invited me to their church, and I was desperate enough to go, and at the church they had a potted ficus they called a Giving Tree, decorated with paper ornaments, each ornament printed with a good deed you could choose.

My ornament said: Take a hospice patient on a date.

That was their word, "date." And there was a phone number.

I took the man with one leg, then him and his mother, all

over the area, to scenic viewpoints, to museums, his wheelchair folded up in the back of my fifteen-year-old Mercury Bobcat. His mother smoking, silent. Her son was thirty years old, and she had two weeks of vacation. At night, I'd take her back to her TravelLodge next to the freeway, and she'd smoke, sitting on the hood of my car, talking about her son already in the past tense. He could play the piano, she said. In school, he earned a degree in music, but ended up demonstrating electric organs in shopping-mall stores.

These were conversations after we had no emotions left.

I was twenty-five years old, and the next day I was back under trucks with maybe three or four hours sleep. Only now my own problems didn't seem very bad. Just looking at my hands and feet, marveling at the weight I could lift, the way I could shout against the pneumatic roar of the shop, my whole life felt like a miracle instead of a mistake.

In two weeks the mother was gone home. In another three months, her son was gone. Dead, gone. I drove people with cancer to see the ocean for their last time. I drove people with AIDS to the top of Mount Hood so they could see the whole world while there was still time.

I sat bedside while the nurse told me what to look for at the moment of death, the gasping and unconscious struggle of someone drowning in their sleep as renal failure filled their lungs with water. The monitor would beep every five or ten seconds as it injected morphine into the patient. The patient's eyes would roll back, bulging and entirely white. You held their cold hand for hours, until another escort came to the rescue, or until it didn't matter.

The mother in Wisconsin sent me an afghan she'd crocheted, purple and red. Another mother or grandmother I'd escorted sent me an afghan in blue, green, and white. Another came in red, white, and black. Granny squares, zigzag patterns. They piled up at one end of the couch until my housemates asked if we could store them in the attic.

Just before he'd died, the woman's son, the man with one leg, just before he'd lost consciousness, he'd begged me to go into his old apartment. There was a closet full of sex toys. Magazines. Dildos. Leatherwear. It was nothing he wanted his mother to find, so I promised to throw it all out.

So I went there, to the little studio apartment, sealed and stale after months empty. Like a crypt, I'd say, but that's not the right word. It sounds too dramatic. Like cheesy organ music. But in fact, just sad.

The sex toys and anal whatnots were just sadder. Orphaned. That's not the right word either, but it's the first word that comes to mind.

The afghans are still boxed and in my attic. Every Christmas a housemate will go look for ornaments and find the afghans, red and black, green and purple, each one a dead person, a son or daughter or grandchild, and whoever finds them will ask if we can use them on our beds or give them to Goodwill.

And every Christmas I'll say no. I can't say what scares me more, throwing away all these dead children or sleeping with them.

Don't ask me why, I tell people. I refuse to even talk about it. That was all ten years ago. I sold the Bobcat in 1989. I quit being an escort.

Maybe because after the man with one leg, after he died, after his sex toys were all garbage-bagged, after they were buried in the Dumpster, after the apartment windows were open and the smell of leather and latex and shit was gone, the apartment looked good. The sofa bed was a tasteful mauve, the walls and carpet, cream. The little kitchen had butcher-block countertops. The bathroom was all white and clean.

I sat there in the tasteful silence. I could've lived there.

Anyone could've lived there.

{Almost California}

The infection on my shaved head is finally starting to heal when I get the package in the mail today.

Here's the screenplay based on my first novel, *Fight Club*.

It's from 20th Century Fox. The agent in New York said this would happen. It's not like I wasn't warned. I was even a little part of the process. I went down to Los Angeles and sat through two days of story conferences where we jerked the plot around. The people at 20th Century Fox got me a room at the Century Plaza. We drove through the studio backlot. They pointed out Arnold Schwarzenegger. My hotel room had a giant whirlpool tub, and I sat in the middle of it and waited most of an hour for it to fill enough that I could turn on the bubble jets. In my hand was my little bottle of mini-bar gin.

The infection on my head was from the day before I was going to Hollywood. I was getting flown to LAX, so what I did is run down to the Gap and try to buy a pumpkin-colored polo shirt. The idea was to look Southern Californian.

The infection was from not reading the directions on a tube of men's depilatory. This is like Nair or Neet, but extra-strong, for black men to shave their faces with.

Right on the tube of Magic brand men's depilatory, it says in all caps: DO NOT USE WITH A RAZOR. This is even underlined. The infection was not the fault of the package designers at Magic. Fast-forward to me sitting in my Century Plaza whirlpool tub. Water rushes in, but the tub is so big that even after half an hour, I'm just sitting there with my gin and my shaved head with my butt in a little puddle of warm water. The walls of the tub are marble, chilled to ice-cold by the air conditioning. The little almond soaps are already packed in my suitcase.

The check from the movie option is already in my bank account.

The bathroom is lined with huge mirrors and indirect lighting, so I can see myself from every angle, naked and wallowing in an inch of water with my drink getting warm. This is everything I wanted to make real. The whole time you're writing, some less-than-Zen little polyp of your brain wants to be flying first-class to LAX. You want to pose for book-jacket photos. You want for there to be a media escort standing at the gate when you get off the plane, and you want to be chauffeured, not delivered, but chauffeured from dazzling interview to glittering book-signing event.

This is the dream. Admit it. Probably, you'd be more shallow than that. Probably, you'd want to be trading toenail secrets with Demi Moore in the green room just before you go onstage as a guest on the David Letterman show.

Yeah. Well, welcome to the market for literary fiction.

Your book has about a hundred days on the bookstore shelf before it's an official failure.

After that, the stores start returning the books to your publisher and prices start to fall. Books don't move. Books go to the shredder.

Your little chunk of your heart, the little first novel you wrote, your heart gets slashed 70 percent, and still nobody wants it.

Then you find yourself at the Gap trying on pastel knit shirts and squinting when you look in the mirror so you look almost good. Almost California. There's the movie deal to support—your hope is, now, that will save your book. Just because a big publisher is doing my first novel, that doesn't make me attractive. Lazy and stupid come to mind. When it comes to being attractive and fun to be around, I just can't compete. Stepping off the airplane in Los Angeles with my hair sprayed and wearing a salmon-colored polo shirt was not going to help.

Having the publicist at the big publishing house call everybody and tell them I was attractive and fun was only going to give people false hope.

The only thing worse than showing up at LAX ugly is showing up ugly but showing signs that you really tried to look good. You gave it your best effort but this is the best you could do. Your hair's cut and skin's tanned, your teeth are flossed and the hair in your nose is tweezed, but you still look ugly. You're wearing a 100 percent cotton casual knit shirt from the Gap. You gargled. You used eyedrops and deodorant, but you still come off the plane missing a few chromosomes.

That wasn't going to happen to me.

The idea was to make sure nobody thought I was even trying to look good. The idea was to wear the clothes I wore every day. To remove any risk of failed hairstyling, I'd shave my head.

This wasn't the first time I'd shaved my head. Most of the time I was writing *Fight Club* I had that blue, shaved-head look. Then, what can I say, my hair grew back. It was cold. I had hair when it came time to take my book-jacket photo, not that hair helped.

Even when they took my picture for the jacket, the photographer made it clear the pictures would turn out ugly, and it was not her fault.

So I left all the new colors of polo shirts including pumpkin, terra cotta, saffron, and celadon at the Gap, and I went and didn't read the directions on a tube of men's depilatory. I frosted my head with the stuff, and I started to hack at my scalp with a razor. The only thing worse you could do is get water mixed in the depilatory. So I ran hot water over my head.

Imagine your head slashed with razor cuts and then throwing lye on the cuts.

Tomorrow, I was going to Hollywood. That night, I couldn't get my head to stop bleeding. Little bits of toilet paper were stuck all over my swelled-up scalp. It was a sort of papier-mâché look, with my brains inside. I felt better when my head started to scab, but then the red parts were still swollen. The blue stubble of hair started pushing up from underneath scabs. The ingrown hairs made little whiteheads I had to squeeze.

It was: The Elephant Man goes to Hollywood.

The people at the airline hustled me onboard, fast, like a donor organ. When I reclined my seat back, my scabs stuck to the little paper headrest cover. After our touchdown, the flight attendant had to peel it off. This probably wasn't the peak experience of *her* day, either.

This is why I write.

The infected head thing just got worse. Everyone meeting me looked legendary, like all the guys were JFK Jr. All the women were Uma Thurman. At all the restaurants we went to, execs from Warner Brothers and Tri-Star would come over and talk about their latest project.

This is *so* why I write.

Nobody made the mistake of eye contact with me. They all talked about the latest buzz.

The producer for the *Fight Club* movie drove me around the Fox backlot. We saw where they filmed *NYPD Blue*. I said how I didn't watch television. This was not the best news to let slip.

We went to the Malibu Colony. We went to Venice Beach. The one place I wanted to go was the Getty Museum, but you have to book an appointment a month in advance.

So this is why I write. Because most times, your life isn't funny the first time through. Most times, you can hardly stand it.

My head would just bleed and bleed. Whoever was lowest in the pecking order, I had to ride in their car. They showed me those concrete hand- and footprints, and they stood off to one side discussing the grosses for *Twister* and *Mission: Impossible* while I wandered around the same as the rest of the tourists with their heads bowed looking for Marilyn Monroe.

They drove me through Brentwood and Bel-Air and Beverly Hills and Pacific Palisades.

They left me at the hotel where I had two hours before I had to be ready for dinner. There I was, and there was the mini-bar just asking to be violated, and there was a bathroom bigger than where I live. The bathroom was lined with mirror, and everywhere, there I was, all naked with the eruptions on my head finally draining clear liquid. The little hotel gin bottle in my hand. The gigantic bathtub kept filling and filling, but never got more than an inch deep.

All those years you write and write. You sit in the dark and say, someday. A book contract. A jacket photo. A book tour. A Hollywood movie. And someday you get them, and it's not how you planned.

Then you get the screenplay for your book in the mail, and it says: "*Fight Club* by Jim Uhls." He's the screenwriter. Way underneath that, in parentheses, it says: Based on the novel by you.

That's why I write, because life never works except in retrospect. And writing makes you look back. Because since you can't control life, at least you can control your version. Because even sitting in my puddle of warm Los Angeles water, I was already thinking what I'd tell my friends when they asked about this trip. I'd tell them all about my infection and Malibu and the bottomless bathtub, and they'd say:

You should write that down.

{The Lip Enhancer}

It was Ina who first told me about Brad's lips, and what he does with them. We'd met Brad this last summer, near Los Angeles, in San Pedro, on six acres of barren concrete with gang warfare, Crip and Blood territory staked out all around us. It was the set for a movie based on a book I'd written and could barely remember. Just before this, a neighborhood man had been tied to a bus stop bench here. The set crews found him, tied up, shot to death. The crew was building a rotting Victorian mansion for a million dollars.

All this buildup, this scene setting is so I don't look too stupid.

This will only look like it's about Brad Pitt.

It was one or two o'clock in the morning when Ina and I got

there. At the production base camp, movie extras slept in dark lumps, curled up inside their cars. Waiting for their call. When we parked, a security guard explained how we'd have to walk unprotected for the last two blocks to the actual movie shooting location.

A pop, then another pop came from the dark neighborhood nearby.

Drive-by shootings, the guard told us. To get to the set, he said, we needed to keep our heads down and run. Just run, he said. Now.

So we ran.

According to Ina, what Brad does is lick his lips. A lot. According to Ina, this is probably not accidental. According to Ina, Brad has great lips.

Somewhere along the line my sister sent me a videotape of Oprah Winfrey, and there was Brad being interviewed, and Ina was pretty much right all over.

The first day we met Brad, he ran up with his shirt open, tanned and smiling, and said, "Thank you for the best fucking part of my whole fucking career!"

That's about all I remember.

That, and I wanted to have lips.

Big lips are everywhere. Fashion models, movie stars. Where I live in Oregon, in a house in the woods, you can ignore a lot of the world, but one day we got a mail-order catalogue and there inside was the Lip Enhancer.

For this movie, Brad had the caps knocked off his front teeth and chipped, snaggle-tooth caps glued on. He shaved his head. Between takes, the wardrobe people rubbed his clothes in the dust on the ground. And he still looked so good Ina couldn't put two words together. Girls from the 'hood stood five deep at the barricades two blocks away and chanted his name.

I had to get me some of those lips.

According to the people at Facial Sculpting, Inc., you can get collagen lip injections, but they don't last. Full collagen lips will run you around $6,880 per year. Plus, collagen tends to move around inside, giving you lumpy lips. Plus, the injection process causes dark bruising and swelling that can last up to a week, with new collagen injections needed every month.

To be fair, I called five local cosmetic surgeons in Oregon, all of whom do lips, all of whom refused to even discuss the Lip Enhancer. Even when I agreed to pay a hundred-dollar consultation fee. Even when I got down and begged.

Oh, Dr. Linda Mueller, you know who you are.

The Lip Enhancer cost me $25, plus a couple bucks for shipping, plus the snide tone of the man who took my order. It's not really marketed to men. We're supposed to be above all that. Still, the Lip Enhancer is similar to a huge number of penis enlargement systems you can buy.

These are systems you can buy, and use, and write funny silly essays about and therefore tax-deduct; needless to say, several of those systems are now in the mail to me.

The key word is "suction." Like those penis systems, the Lip Enhancer uses gentle suction to distend your lips. Basically, it's a two-piece telescoping tube, sealed at one end. You place the open end of the tube against your lips, then pull the sealed end away from you, lengthening the tube. This creates the suction that pulls your lips inside the tube, giving you full, pouty lips in about two minutes.

In the instructions, the lovely young woman has her lips sucked so far into the clear tube that she looks like a kissing gourami fish.

Some people, it gives them a big hickey around their mouth. This is just like when you were a kid and you pressed a plastic glass around your mouth and chin and sucked all the air out until you had a huge dark bruise that looked like the five-o'clock shadow of Fred Flintstone or Homer Simpson.

You should not use the Lip Enhancer if you're a diabetic or have any blood disorder.

According to the catalogue, your new big full pouty lips will last about six hours.

This is how Cinderella must've felt.

There are similar suction systems to give you bigger, more perky nipples.

In the near future, you can imagine, every big evening will begin hours earlier with you getting sucked on by different appliances, each of them making some part of you bigger for a few hours. The whole evening would then be a race to get naked and accomplish some lovin' before your parts snapped back to their original size.

Yes, there's even a system for enlarging your testicles.

I was visitor number 921 to the Lip Enhancer website.

I was visitor number 500,000 to any of the penis enlargement sites.

Your first week with the Lip Enhancer, you have to condition your lips twice a day. This involves short, gentle sessions of getting your lips sucked. This is less exciting than it sounds.

Now, I've kissed thin lips, and I've kissed thick lips. Me, I have what you'd call combination lips, a large lower lip and pretty much no upper lip. Some cultures scar their faces with knives. Some flatten the heads of their babies with special cradle boards. Some distend their necks with wire coils. All these *National Geographic* images went through my mind as I sat in my car, my head tilted back at the recommended forty-five-degree angle, the Lip Enhancer tight around my mouth and my lips sucked into the tube. Beauty is a construct of the culture. A mutually agreed upon standard. Nobody used to look at George Washington, with his wooden teeth, in his powdered wig, and say, Fashion Victim.

After two minutes—the recommended maximum treatment time—I did not look like Brad. Trying to talk, I pronounced almost all my consonants as B's, the same vaguely racist way the character with the huge lips used to talk in the old *Fat Albert* cartoons on Saturday morning.

"Hey'b, Fab Alberb," I said to the rearview mirror. "How'b boub dees'b libs?"

My lips felt raw and swollen, as if I'd eaten barrels of salty popcorn.

I could see why none of the lovely models in the Lip Enhancer brochures ever smiled.

I hurried out of the car, still in the window of time before my lips would shrink back to nothing. Back to just the regular, ordinary me. I went to a writers' workshop, and my friend Tom asked, "Didn't you use to have a mustache?"

I tried licking them à la Brad on *Oprah*.

My friend Erin leaned close, squinted hard, and asked, "Have you had dental work done today?"

I remembered Brad in the dentist's chair, sitting through the whole pain of getting his caps switched, to glam down his look with new broken teeth. How one day he had to have good teeth, and the next day, breaks and chips. How every switch meant more time under the dentist. More pain.

It's funny, but you see yourself in a certain way, and any change is hard to understand. It's hard to say if I looked better or worse. To me it was creepy, like those ads in old comic books where you could send away for "nigger lips" and "Jew noses." A caricature of something. In this case, a caricature of beauty.

According to the package enclosures, you can wash the Lip

Enhancer with soap and water. According to the website, it makes a great gift. So now it's washed and wrapped, and Ina's birthday is October 16.

Somewhere in the mail, in the backs of trucks or the bellies of airplanes, various other suction systems are still headed my way. Ten of thousands are headed for other people. Me, these people, we believe. Something will save us. Deliver us. Make us happy. And, sure, you could say this kind of special effect is okay for an actor. An actor is playing a role. Well, I would say, who isn't?

So this wasn't really about Brad.

It's about everybody.

{Monkey Think, Monkey Do}

This summer a young man pulled me aside in a bookstore and said he loved how in *Fight Club* I wrote about waiters tainting food. He asked me to sign a book and said he worked in a five-star restaurant where they monkey with celebrities' food all the time.

"Margaret Thatcher," he said, "has eaten my sperm." He held up one hand, fingers spread, and said, "At least five times."

Writing that book, I knew a movie projectionist who collected single frames from porno movies and made them into slides. When I talked to people about cutting these frames into G-rated family movies, one friend said, "Don't. People will read that, and they'll start doing it . . ."

Later, when they were shooting the *Fight Club* movie, some

Hollywood big names told me the book hit home because they, themselves, had spliced porno into movies as angry teenage projectionists. People told me about blowing their noses into hamburgers at fast-food cooking jobs. They told me about changing the bottles of hair dye from box to box in the drugstore, blond to black, red to brown, and coming back to see angry, wild-dyed people screaming at the store manager. This was the decade of "transgressive novels," starting early with *American Psycho* and continuing with *Trainspotting* and *Fight Club*. These were novels about bored bad boys who'd try anything to feel alive. Everything people told me, I could roll it into a book and sell.

On every book tour, people told me how each time they sat in the emergency exit row on an airplane, the whole flight would be a struggle not to pop open that door. The air sucking out of the plane, the oxygen masks falling, the screaming chaos and "Mayday! Mayday!" emergency landing, it was all so clear. That door, so begging to be opened.

The Danish philosopher Søren Kierkegaard defines dread as the knowledge of what you must do to prove you're free, even if it will destroy you. His example is Adam in the Garden of Eden, happy and content until God shows him the Tree of Knowledge and says, "Don't eat this." Now Adam is no longer free. There is one rule he can break, he *must* break, to prove his freedom, even if it destroys him. Kierkegaard says the moment we are forbidden to do something, we will do it. It is inevitable.

Monkey think, monkey do.

According to Kierkegaard, the person who allows the law to control his life, who says the possible isn't possible because it is illegal, is leading an inauthentic life.

In Portland, Oregon, someone is filling tennis balls with

matchheads and taping them shut. They leave the balls on the street for anyone to find, and any kick or throw will make them explode. So far, a man's lost a foot; a dog, its head.

Now the graffiti taggers are using acid glass-etching creams to write on shop and car windows. At suburban Tigard High School, an unidentified teenage boy takes his shit and wipes it around the walls of the men's bathroom. The school knows him only as the "Una-Pooper." Nobody's supposed to talk about him because the school is afraid of copycats.

As Kierkegaard would say, every time we see what's possible, we make it happen. We make it inevitable. Until Stephen King wrote about high school losers killing their peer groups, school shootings were unknown. But did *Carrie* and *Rage* make it inevitable?

Millions of us paid money to watch the Empire State Building destroyed in *Independence Day*. Now the Department of Defense has enrolled the best Hollywood creative people to brainstorm terrorist scenarios, including director David Fincher, who made the Century City skyline fall down in *Fight Club*. We want to know every way we might be attacked. So we can be prepared.

Because of Ted Kaczynski, the Unabomber, you can't mail a package without going to a post office clerk. Because of people dropping bowling balls onto freeways, we have fences enclosing highway overpasses.

All of this reaction, as if we can protect ourselves against everything.

This summer, Dale Shackleford, the man convicted of killing my father, said: Hey, the state could give him the death penalty, but he and his white-supremacist friends had built and buried several anthrax bombs around Spokane, Washington. If the state killed him, someday a backhoe would rupture a buried bomb and tens of thousands would die. Among themselves, the prosecution team started calling this kind of statement a "Shackle-Freudian lie."

What's coming is a million new reasons not to live your life. You can deny your possibility to succeed and blame it on something else. You can fight against everything—Margaret Thatcher, property owners, the urge to open that door mid-flight . . . everything you pretend keeps you down. You can live Kierkegaard's inauthentic life. Or you can make what Kierkegaard called your Leap of Faith, where you stop living as a reaction to circumstances and start living as a force for what you say should be.

What's coming is a million new reasons to go ahead.

What's going out is the cathartic transgressive novel.

Movies like *Thelma and Louise*, books like *The Monkey Wrench Gang*, their audience is less likely to laugh and understand. For the time being, we get to pretend we're not our own worst enemy.

{Brinksmanship}

In this one bar, you couldn't set your beer bottle on the table or cockroaches would climb up the label and drown themselves.

Anytime you set down a beer, you'd have a dead cockroach in your next mouthful. There were Filipino strippers who came out between their sets to shoot pool in string bikinis. For five dollars, they'd pull a plastic chair into the shadows between stacked cases of beer and lap dance you.

We used to go there because it was near Good Samaritan Hospital.

We'd visit Alan until his pain medication put him to sleep, then Geoff and I would go drink beer. Geoff, grinding his beer bottle on roach after roach as they ran across our table.

We'd talk to the strippers. We talked to guys at other tables.

We were young, young-ish, late twenties, and one night a wait-ress asked us, "If you're already watching dancers in a dive like this, what will you be doing when you're old men?"

At the next table was a doctor, an older man who explained a lot of things. He said how the stage was spotlighted with red and black lights because they hid the bruises and needle marks on the dancers. He showed how their fingernails, their hair and eyes told their childhood diseases. Their teeth and skin showed how well they ate. Their breath in your face, the smell of their sweat could tell you how they'd probably die.

In that bar, the floor, tables, the chairs, everything was sticky. Someone said Madonna went there a lot when she was in Portland filming *Body of Evidence,* but by then I'd quit going. By then Alan and his cancer were both dead.

It's a story I've told before, but I once promised to introduce a friend to Brad Pitt if she'd let me assist in dissecting some medical-school cadavers.

She'd failed premed three times already, but her father was a doctor so she just kept going back. She was my age now, middle-aged, the oldest premed in her class, and all night we dissected three cadavers so first-year students could examine them the next day.

Inside each body was a country I'd always heard about but never thought I'd visit. Here was the spleen and the heart and liver. Inside the head was the hypothalamus, the plaques and tangles of Alzheimer's. Still, I was most amazed by what wasn't there. These yellow, shaved, and leathery bodies were so differ-ent from my friend who used her saws and knives. For the first time, I saw that maybe human beings are more than their bod-ies. That maybe there is a soul.

The night she met Brad, we walked out of soundstage 15 on

the Fox lot. It was after midnight, and we walked through the dark standing New York sets used in a million productions since they were built for Barbra Streisand in *Hello, Dolly!* A taxi passed us with New York license plates. Steam rose from fake manhole covers. Now the sidewalks were full of people in winter coats, carrying shopping bags from Gumps and Bloomingdales. In another minute, someone waved to stop us from walking—us laughing and wearing shorts and T-shirts—into a Christmas episode of *NYPD Blue.*

We walked another way, past an open soundstage where spotlighted actors in blue surgical scrubs leaned over an operating table and pretended to save someone's life.

This other time, I was scrubbing the kitchen floor and pulled a muscle in my side. That's how it felt at first.

For the next three days, I'd go to the urinal and not pee, and by the time I left work and drove to the doctor's office, the pain had me duck-walking. By then, the doctor from the strip bar was my doctor. He felt my back and said, "You need to get to the hospital or you're going to lose this kidney."

A few days later, I called him from the bathtub, where I'm sitting in a puddle of piss and blood, drinking California champagne and popping Vicodins. On the phone, I tell him, "I passed my stone," and in my other hand is a nine-millimeter ball of tiny oxalic acid crystals, all of them razor-sharp.

The next day, I flew to Spokane and accepted an award from the Pacific Northwest Booksellers Association for *Fight Club.*

The week after, on the day of my follow-up appointment, someone called to say the doctor was dead. A heart attack in the night, and he died alone, on the floor, next to his bed.

My fiberglass bathtub still has a blood-red ring around it.

The black and red lights. The standing sets. The embalmed cadavers. My doctor, my friend, dead on his bedroom floor. I want to believe they're all just stories now. Our physical bodies, I want to believe that they're all just props. That life, physical life, is an illusion.

And I do believe it, but only for a moment at a time.

It's funny, but the last time I saw my father alive was at my brother-in-law's funeral. He was young, my brother-in-law, young-ish, in his late forties, when he had the stroke. The church gave us a menu and said to choose two hymns, a psalm, and three prayers. It was like ordering a Chinese dinner.

My sister came out of the viewing room, from her private viewing of her husband's body, and she waved our mother inside, saying, "There's been a mistake."

This thing in the casket, drained and dressed and painted, looked nothing like Gerard. My sister said, "That's not him."

This last time I saw my father, he handed me a blue-striped tie and asked how to tie it. I told him to hold still. With his collar turned, I looped the tie around his neck and started tying it. I told him, "Look up."

It was the opposite of the moment when he'd shown me the trick of the rabbit running around the cave and he'd tied my first pair of shoes.

That was the first time in decades my family had gone to mass together.

While I'm writing this, my mother calls to say my grandfather's had a series of strokes. He's unable to swallow, and his lungs are filling with fluid. A friend, maybe my best friend, calls to say he has lung cancer. My grandfather's five hours away. My friend's across town. Me, I have work to do.

The waitress used to say, "What will you be doing when you're old men?"

I used to tell her, "I'll worry about that when I get there."

If I get there.

I'm writing this piece right on deadline.

My brother-in-law used to call this behavior "brinksmanship," the tendency to leave things until the last moment, to imbue them with more drama and stress and appear the hero by racing the clock.

"Where I was born," Georgia O'Keeffe used to say, "and where and how I have lived is unimportant."

She said, "It is what I have done with where I have been that should be of any interest."

I'm sorry if this all seems a little rushed and desperate.

It is.

{ Now I Remember . . . }

Item: Twenty-seven boxes of Valentine's candy, cost $298.

Item: Fourteen talking robotic birds, cost $112.

As April 15 gets closer and closer, my tax preparer, Mary, keeps calling, asking, "What is *this* all about?"

Item: Two nights at the Carson Hilton in Carson, California, February 21, 2001.

Mary asks, why was I in Carson? The twenty-first is my birthday. What about this trip makes it a business deduction?

The Valentine's candy, the talking birds, the nights in the Carson Hilton, they make me so glad I keep receipts. Otherwise I'd have no idea. A year later, I have no memory about what these items represent.

That's why, the moment I saw Guy Pearce in *Memento*, I

knew finally someone was telling my story. Here was a movie about the predominant art form of our time:

Note taking.

All my friends with PalmPilots and cell phones, they're always calling themselves and leaving reminders to themselves about what's about to happen. We leave Post-it notes for ourselves. We go to that shop in the mall, the one where they engrave whatever shit you want on a silver-plated box or a fountain pen, and we get a reminder for every special event that life goes by too fast for us to remember. We buy those picture frames where you record a message on a sound chip. We videotape everything! Oh, and now there's those digital cameras, so we can all email around our photos—this century's equivalent of the boring vacation slide show. We organize and reorganize. We record and archive.

I'm not surprised that people like *Memento*. I'm surprised it didn't win every Academy Award and then destroy the entire consumer market for recordable compact discs, blank-page books, Dictaphones, DayTimers, and every other prop we use to keep track of our lives.

My filing system is my fetish. Before I left the Freightliner Corporation, I bought a wall of black steel four-drawer filing cabinets at the office-surplus price of five bucks each. Now, when the receipts pile up, the letters and contracts and whatnot, I close the blinds and put on a compact disc of rain sounds and file, file, file. I use hanging file folders and special color-coded plastic file labels. I am Guy Pearce without the low body fat and good looks. I'm organizing by date and nature of expense. I'm organizing story ideas and odd facts.

This summer, a woman in Palouse, Washington, told me how rapeseed can be grown as a food *or* a lubricant. There are two different varieties of the seed. Unfortunately, the lubricant type is poisonous. Because of this, every county in the nation must choose whether it will allow farmers to grow either the food or the lubricant variety of rapeseed. A few of the wrong type seeds in a county and people could die. She also told me how the people bankrolling the seeming-grassroots movement to tear down dams are really the American coal industry—not environmentalist fish-huggers and white-water rafters, but coal miners who resent hydroelectric power. She knows, she says, because she designs their websites.

Like the robotic birds, these are interesting facts, but what can I do with them?

I can file them. Someday, there will come a use for them. The way my father and grandfather lugged home lumber and wrecked cars, anything free or cheap with a potential future use, I now scribble down facts and figures and file them away for a future project.

Picture Andy Warhol's townhouse, crowded and stacked with kitsch, cookie jars and old magazines, and that's my mind. The files are an annex to my head.

Books are another annex. The books I write are my overflow retention system for stories I can no longer keep in my recent memory. The books I read are to gather facts for more stories. Right now I'm looking at a copy of the *Phaedrus*, a fictional conversation between Socrates and a young Athenian named Phaedrus.

Socrates is trying to convince the young man that speech is better than written communication, or any recorded communication including film. According to Socrates, the god Theuth in ancient Egypt invented numbers and calculation and gambling and geometry and astronomy . . . and Theuth invented writing.

Then he presented his inventions to the great god-king Thamus, asking which of them should be presented to the Egyptian people.

Thamus ruled that writing was a *pharmakon*. Like the word "drug" it could be used for good or bad. It could cure or poison.

According to Thamus, writing would allow humans to extend their memories and share information. But, more important, writing would allow humans to rely too much on these external means of recording. Our own memories would wither and fail. Our notes and records would replace our minds.

Worse than that, written information can't teach, according to Thamus. You can't question it, and it can't defend itself when people misunderstand or misrepresent it. Written communication gives people what Thamus called "the false conceit of knowledge," a fake certainty that they understand something.

So, all those videotapes of your childhood, will they really give you a better understanding of yourself? Or will they just shore up whatever faulty memories you have? Can they replace your ability to sit down and ask your family questions? To learn from your grandparents.

If Thamus were here, I'd tell him that memory itself is a *pharmakon*.

Guy Pearce's happiness is based entirely on his past. He must complete something he can hardly remember. Something that he may even be misremembering because it's too painful.

Me and Guy, we're joined at the hip.

My two nights in Carson, California—looking at the credit-card receipt, I can remember them. Sort of. I was posing for a picture for *GQ* magazine. They'd originally wanted me to lie in a pile of rubber dildos, but we'd reached a compromise. It was the night of the Grammy Awards, so every decent hotel room in L.A. was taken. Another receipt shows it cost me seventy bucks in cab fare just to get to the photo shoot.

Now I remember.

The fashion stylist told me how her Chihuahua could suck its own penis. People loved her dog, until it ran to the center of every party and started honking its own wiener. This had cleared out more than a few parties at her house. The photographer told me horror stories about photographing Minnie Driver and Jennifer Lopez.

At a similar photo shoot for the Abercrombie & Fitch catalogue, the photographer tells me how his Chihuahua has "erectile retraction dysfunction." Whenever the little thing gets a boner, this guy—the Abercrombie photographer—has to reach in and make sure the dog's tiny foreskin isn't too tight.

Oh, now the memories come flooding back.

Now, day and night, foremost in my mind is the message: NEVER GET A CHIHUAHUA.

After the *GQ* photo shoot—where I wore expensive clothes and stood in a movie studio mock-up of an airplane bathroom—a movie producer took me to a beachfront hotel in Santa Monica. The hotel was big and expensive, with a posh bar that looked out at the sun setting over the ocean. It was an hour before the Grammys would start, and beautiful famous people were mingling in evening clothes, having dinner and drinks and calling for their limousines. The sunset, the people, me a little drunk and still wearing my *GQ* makeup, me so professionally art-directed, I'd died and gone to Hollywood heaven—until something dropped onto my plate.

A bobby pin.

I touched my hair and felt dozens of bobby pins, all of them worked halfway out of the hairsprayed mass of my hair. Here in front of music aristocracy, I was a drunken Olive Oyl, bristling with pins and dropping them every time I moved my head.

Funny, but without the receipts, I wouldn't have remembered any of it.

That's what I mean by *pharmakon.* Don't bother to write this down.

{Consolation Prizes}

Another waiter has just served me another free meal because I'm "that guy."

I'm the guy who wrote that book. The *Fight Club* book. Because there's a scene in the book where a loyal waiter, a member of the fight club cult, serves the narrator free food. Where, now in the movie, Edward Norton and Helena Bonham Carter get free food.

Then a magazine editor, another magazine editor, calls me, angry and ranting because he wants to send a writer to the underground fight club in his area.

"It's cool, man," he says from New York. "You can tell me where. We won't screw it up."

I tell him there's no such place. There's no secret society of clubs where guys bash each other and gripe about their empty lives, their hollow careers, their absent fathers. Fight clubs are make-believe. You can't go there. I made them up.

"Okay," he's saying. "Be that way. If you don't trust us, then to hell with you."

Another pack of letters arrive care of my publisher, from young men telling me they've gone to fight clubs in New Jersey and London and Spokane. Telling me about their fathers. In today's mail are wristwatches, lapel pins, and coffee mugs, prizes from hundreds of contests my father enters my siblings and me in every winter.

Parts of *Fight Club* have always been true. It's less a novel than an anthology of my friends' lives. I do have insomnia and wander with no sleep for weeks. Angry waiters I know mess with food. They shave their heads. My friend Alice makes soap. My friend Mike cuts single frames of smut into family features. Every guy I know feels let down by his father.

Even my father feels let down by *his* father.

But now, more and more, what little was fiction is becoming reality.

The night before I mailed the manuscript to an agent in 1995, when it was just a couple hundred sheets of paper, a friend joked that she wanted to meet Brad Pitt.

I joked that I wanted to leave my job as a technical writer who worked on diesel trucks all day.

Now those pages are a movie starring Pitt and Norton and Bonham Carter, directed by David Fincher. Now I'm unemployed.

Twentieth Century Fox let me bring some friends down to the movie shoot, and every morning we ate at the same café in Santa Monica. Every breakfast, we got the same waiter, Charlie, with his movie-star looks and thick hair, until the last morning we were in town. That morning, Charlie walked out of the kitchen with his head shaved. Charlie was in the movie.

My friends who'd been anarchist waiters with shaved heads were now being served eggs by a real waiter who was an actor who was playing a fake anarchist waiter with a shaved head.

It's that same feeling when you get between two mirrors in the barber shop and you can see your reflection of your reflection of your reflection going off into infinity . . .

Now waiters are refusing my money. Editors are grousing. Guys take me aside at bookstore events and beg to know where the local club meets. Women ask, quiet and serious, "Is there a club like this for women?"

A late-night fight club where you can tag some stranger in the crowd and then slug it out until one of you drops . . . ?

These young women say, "Yeah, I really, really need to go to something like that."

A German friend of mine, Carston, learned to speak English in only funny outdated clichés. For him, every party was an "all-singing, all-dancing extravaganza."

Now Carston's clumsy pidgin words are coming out of Brad Pitt's mouth, forty feet high, in front of millions of people. My friend Jeff's trashed ghetto kitchen is re-created in a Hollywood soundstage. The night I went to save my friend Kevin from a Xanax overdose is now Brad rushing to save Helena.

Everything is funnier in retrospect, funnier and prettier and cooler. You can laugh at anything from far enough away.

The story is no longer my story. It's David Fincher's. The set for Edward Norton's yuppie condo is a re-creation of an apartment from David's past. Edward wrote and rewrote his own lines. Brad chipped his teeth and shaved his head. My boss thinks the story is about how he struggles to please *his* demanding boss. My father thought the story was about *his* absent father, my grandfather, who killed his wife and himself with a shotgun.

My father was four in 1943 when he hid under a bed as his parents fought and his twelve brothers and sisters ran into the woods. Then his mother was dead, and his father stomped around the house looking for him, calling for him, still carrying the shotgun.

My father remembers the boots stomping past the bed and the barrel of the shotgun trailing along near the floor. Then he remembers pouring buckets of sawdust on the bodies, to protect them from wasps and flies.

The book, and now the movie, is a product of all these people. And with everything added to it, the fight club story becomes stronger, cleaner, not just the record of one life, but of a generation. Not just of a generation, but of men.

The book is the product of Nora Ephron and Thom Jones and Mark Richard and Joan Didion, Amy Hempel and Bret Ellis and Denis Johnson because those are the people I read.

And now most of my old friends, Jeff and Carston and Alice are moved away, gone, married, dead, graduated, back in school, raising children. This summer, someone murdered my father in the mountains of Idaho and burned his body down to a few pounds of bone. The police say they have no real suspects. He was fifty-nine.

The news came on a Friday morning, through my publicist, who'd been called by the Latah County Sheriff's Office, who'd found me through my publisher on the Internet. The poor publicist, Holly Watson, called me and said, "This might be some kind of sick joke, but you need to call a detective in Moscow, Idaho."

Now here I sit with a table full of food, and you'd think a

free bento and free fish would taste great, but that's not always the case.

I still wander at night.

All that's left is a book, and now a movie, a funny, exciting movie. A wild, excellent movie. What for other people will be a whiplash carnival ride, for my friends and me, is a nostalgic scrapbook. A reminder. Amazing reassuring proof that our anger, our disappointment, our striving and resentment unite us with each other, and now with the world.

What's left is proof we can create reality.

Frieda, the woman who shaved Brad's head, promised me the hair for my Christmas cards, but then she forgot, so I trimmed a friend's golden retriever. Another woman, a friend of my father, calls me, frantic. She's sure the white supremacists killed him, and she wants to "go under deep cover" into their world around Hayden Lake and Butler Lake, in Idaho. She wants me to go along and "act as backup." To "cover her."

So my adventures continue. I will go into the Idaho panhandle. Or I will sit at home like the police want, take Zoloft and wait for them to call.

Or, I don't know.

My father was a sweepstakes junkie, and every week small prizes still arrive in the mail. Wristwatches, coffee mugs, golf towels, calendars, never the big prizes, the cars or boats, these are the little stuff. Another friend, Jennifer, recently lost her father to cancer, and she gets the same kind of little prizes from contests he entered her in months ago. Necklaces, soup mix, taco sauce, and every time one arrives, videogames, toothbrushes, her heart breaks.

Consolation prizes.

A few nights before my father died, he and I talked long

distance for three hours about a tree house he'd built my brother and me. We talked about a batch of chickens I'm raising, how to build them a coop, and if the laying box for each hen should have a wire-mesh floor.

And he said no, a chicken would not shit in its nest.

We talked about the weather, how cold it was at night. He said how in the woods where he lived, the wild turkeys had just hatched their chicks, and he told me how each tom turkey would open its wings at dusk and gather in all its young. Because they were too large for the hen to protect. To keep them warm.

I told him no male animal could ever be that nurturing.

Now my father's dead, and my hens have their nests.

And now it seems that both he and I were wrong.

POSTSCRIPT: The day after Holly Watson called me with the news, my brother was due to arrive from South Africa. He was coming to handle some regular bank and tax details; instead, we drove to Idaho to help identify a body the police said might be our father. The body was found shot, next to the body of a woman, in a burned-down garage in the mountains outside Kendrick, Idaho. This was the summer of 1999. The summer the *Fight Club* movie came out. We went to our father's house in the mountains outside of Spokane, trying to track down some X-rays that showed the two vertebrae fused in Dad's back after a railroad accident left him disabled.

My father's place in the mountains was beautiful, hundreds of acres, wild turkeys and moose and deer everywhere. On the road up to the house, there was a new sign. It was next to a boulder that lay beside the road. It said, "Kismet Rock." We had no idea what the sign meant.

Before my brother and I could find the X-rays, the police

called to say the body was Dad's. They'd used dental records we'd shipped to them earlier.

At the trial for the man who murdered him, Dale Shackleford, it came out that my father had answered a personals ad placed by a woman who's ex-husband had threatened to kill her and any man that he ever found her with. The heading of the personals ad was "Kismet." My father was one of five men who answered it. He was the one she chose.

According to Latah County detectives, Shackleford claimed I was harassing him, sending him copies of the *Fight Club* movie. This was in January 2000, when the only copies were Academy Award screening copies.

This was the dead woman found beside my father, the woman who placed the ad, Donna Fontaine. This was only their second or third date. She and my father had gone to her home to feed some animals before driving to my father's house where he was going to surprise her with the "Kismet Rock" sign. A sort of landmark named for their new relationship.

Her ex-husband was waiting and followed them up the driveway. According to the court's verdict, he killed them and set fire to their bodies in the garage. They'd known each other for less than two months.

Dale Shackleford is appealing his death sentence.

About the Author

Chuck Palahniuk's six novels are the bestselling *Diary, Lullaby, Fight Club,* which was made into a film by director David Fincher, *Survivor, Invisible Monsters,* and *Choke.* He is also the author of the nonfiction profile of Portland, *Fugitives and Refugees,* published as part of the Crown Journeys series. He lives in the Pacific North-west.